TRUMPET OF SALVATION

TRUMPET of
SALVATION

The Story of William and Catherine Booth

by
NORMAN E. NYGAARD

ZONDERVAN PUBLISHING HOUSE
GRAND RAPIDS   MICHIGAN

To the
multitude of soldiers,
men and women of every race
and nation
in the Salvation Army

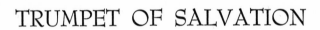

TRUMPET OF SALVATION

CHAPTER 1

The congregation of Wesley Chapel in Nottingham, England, good, substantial, respectable citizens, middle class for the most part, the men decently attired in broadcloth, the women in rustling bombazine, were comfortably settled in their conventional auditorium, prepared to listen to a comfortable sermon. It was a rainy day in the winter of 1845 and they had shaken the water from their umbrellas and left them in the entry.

They were kind, complacent folk. They had nodded politely to their friends as they came from the vestibule, and received courteous nods in return. Their minister, in black frock coat, was standing back of the pulpit, prepared to announce the opening hymn when into the sanctuary strode young William Booth, sixteen years of age, tall, erect, with long aquiline nose and piercing brown eyes. Following him came a motley collection of unwashed humanity such as had never before been seen in those hallowed precincts.

Thomas Partridge turned to his wife.

"The young man has gone too far," he whispered. "This is unthinkable."

But his wife couldn't answer. The assorted odors which were wafted into the sanctuary in the wake of the tattered army were more than she could bear. Her nose was covered with a handkerchief which made whispering impossible. The mouths of other staid worshipers popped open and then were closed with equal dispatch.

The minister's face turned pale but sixteen-year-old William was in his element. He showed a blowzy fishwife, with scales still clinging to her leather apron, to a pew with the gallantry of a knight. One of his other charges was suckling an infant at her breast. He seated her next to the Partridges. Other staid burghers had to share their pews with ragged adults and urchins. Toes peeped out of shapeless shoes. There was a general sniffling, and noses were wiped on dirty coats.

William Booth sang lustily on the first hymn. He was altogether happy. His Lord had commanded him in the Scriptures to "go out into the highways and byways and compel them to come in." The only compulsion which he had employed had been that of his intense personality, his winsome, eager invitation, and dire warnings of hell-fire if those who had accompanied him to the chapel persisted in failing to attend church.

He was particularly happy because he was bringing these people to the Methodists, to his own religious group. He was confident that the Methodists could do more for the immortal souls of his charges than could the staid Presbyterians or the worldly Anglicans. To young William the Wesleys were the truest exponents of the Gospel of Christ. The Wesleys, in their lifetime, had been earnest evangelists, and for some months he had been following in their footsteps, preaching on street corners to any company of ragged youths or oldsters who would listen to his messages.

But the service in Wesley Chapel that morning became an embarrassment. The minister stumbled in his preaching. The church officers sat ramrod-straight in their pews, inwardly seething, resolved that this brash lad who, they decided, must be responsible for this unhallowed invasion, should be adequately rebuked for his part in the awful affair.

However, William was oblivious to everything. He had been about his Father's business, and he knew that his Father God, and his Saviour, Jesus Christ, would surely approve the program of mass evangelism which he was initiating. Somehow the service eventually came to a close. The staid members, heads high in the air, departed; William's contingent also quietly made its exit, most of his company sensing the fact that they had not been welcome guests of the members of Wesley Chapel that morning.

The church officers could scarcely wait to make plans to stop the young evangelist from letting his enthusiasm exceed his discretion. Before the Rev. Mr. John Savage left for the parsonage after the service it had been decided that the church officers would meet that same afternoon to discuss the situation. Promptly at three o'clock they convened in the minister's home.

Mr. Savage was inclined to be tolerant.

"William is preaching to such as these nightly," he explained. "He scarcely has time to sleep. With youthful enthusiasm he evidently decided to invite these people to come to church with him. He intended no wrong thereby. It was thoughtless, to be sure, but there was not a spark of malice in the deed."

"But to bring them to our church!" sputtered one of the

stewards. "Why should our church be the one to entertain such . . . such . . . ruffians?"

"Because William is a member of our group," the Rev. Mr. Savage remarked. "And he is a thoroughly consecrated young man."

"Granted that he is an exemplary youth," one of the other stewards interposed, "it must not happen again."

"But how can we stop it?" asked another.

"Summon him to appear before us," the first one said.

"For disciplinary action?" asked Mr. Savage incredulously. "His deed was not one to merit punishment."

"I didn't have that in mind," the steward remarked, "but certainly it would not be improper to counsel the lad."

"Oh, to be sure, that would not be amiss," the Rev. Mr. Savage agreed.

It was decided, therefore, to hold another meeting on Monday evening to remonstrate with William. Frank Powell was selected to call upon young Booth and invite him to come to the session. Powell was a kind old man and it was decided that he would be the best emissary of the board. Powell called at his home on Sunday afternoon but was purposely evasive concerning the purpose of the meeting.

William set off for the church on Monday evening with a light heart, confident that the stewards intended to commend him for his keen interest in evangelism and for having brought to the service so many potential candidates for membership.

He was certain in his own mind that he had not brought them to church for self-gratification. Statistics never interested him: people did. Yet he could not but have a warm feeling in his heart to know that the leaders of his own church were evidently about to recognize his consecrated efforts for the Lord.

The pastor introduced the topic for discussion.

"We have met tonight especially to consider the character of the group which accompanied you to our service yesterday, William," he announced. "We do not question the purity of your motives nor would there have been any objection on the part of our members if you had brought with you a handful of people, but the exceedingly large number who came almost overwhelmed us."

Clarence Nettleton interposed, "Yes, and the stink of their bodies completely did so."

"Never have I seen so many unwashed, ragged, dirty scoundrels in the house of the Lord as came yesterday," Rodney

11

Crawford added. "My wife was altogether sick when we reached home after the service."

William's face paled. This was totally unexpected.

"But the very reason for the existence of the church is to bring souls into the Kingdom," William quietly replied.

"True. But the bodies which house those souls should, at least, be clean," Nettleton retorted.

"But how can they be clean?" William countered. "Those people live in hovels. What money they earn is spent for liquor. Many of them are drunkards. As I have preached to them of nights many could scarcely stand up, so intoxicated were they."

"Yet you would invite them to come to the Lord's house," Frank Powell remarked reproachfully.

"Where else would they find their Lord and Saviour?" William asked, adding as an afterthought, "Besides, I told them when I invited them to come that they would have to be stone sober — and they all were."

"Granted that they were not inebriated," Nettleton remarked. "They still smelled."

"What I'd like to know," Crawford demanded aggressively, "is why they hadn't found the Lord somewhere and at some time before they came to Wesley Chapel."

"But many did," William objected. "They found Him on the street in some of our meetings. I had hoped that they might want to join a church. I wanted them to see what the interior of a church was like. Many had never attended a church service before."

"Could you not have taken them to a larger church? Perhaps to the cathedral?" Nettleton suggested.

"The atmosphere in a cathedral is woefully cold," William objected. "Nor can my people easily accustom themselves to use a prayer book. Many can scarcely read. Our church is so warm, our people so tenderhearted, that I felt certain these folks would be welcomed with open arms."

"If we had so welcomed them we'd have been picking lice out of our hair for a week," Nettleton remarked dryly. "And I still don't have the smell out of the clothing that I wore to church yesterday."

"But the Lord bade me bring them," William replied. "It is not enough that they hear preaching in the street. The psalmist said, 'I was glad when they said unto me, let us go into the house of the Lord.'"

12

"That is not a text for them," Crawford objected. "It is a text for believing Christians."

William, dismayed, looked about the circle. He could not recognize in the grim faces which confronted him the kindly men whom he had known before. This seemed to be an entirely different company. Yet these men had been accounted his friends. When they knew that he planned to spend evening after evening preaching to crowds in the streets they had encouraged him. He could not believe that they seriously objected to his mission.

"What is to happen to these poor folk?" he inquired. "They have souls just as we do. They are sinners as we all are. They need the Saviour more than any of you do because they have been so deeply enmeshed in sin. They need to know the Christ whom we serve."

"True," Nettleton agreed, "but our chapel is scarcely the place where they should be expected to find God. Ours is a respectable place of worship."

"Respectability!" William exploded. "Is that more important than salvation?"

The men looked uncomfortably at one another.

Frank Powell interposed in kindly fashion, "No, William, it is not. We could almost agree with you save that we also believe that respectability accompanies salvation. Do your people all have to be as dirty and as ragged as they were last Sabbath?"

"If they could earn better wages, no," William agreed. "If they had enough to live on, certainly not. But for many of them it is a struggle just to remain alive."

"We can appreciate that," Mr. Powell remarked, "and we would not want to forbid your good people to come to church. But would it not be possible to have them come in smaller numbers? And, in order that they should not disturb our regular members, could they not come in by a separate entrance?"

"There is that door back of the pulpit," the Rev. Mr. Savage suggested. "If they would enter there we could arrange for them to be seated where their body odors would not be wafted in the direction of our people."

"The Lord is no respecter of persons," William asserted positively.

"Of course not," Mr. Savage agreed placatingly. "Nor do we desire so to be. It is merely that these two congregations

13

do not easily blend." He added with a smile, "They are like oil and water."

William bowed his head.

"It shall be as you say," he said. "But I doubt if they will ever return if they feel that they are not welcome."

"Undoubtedly it would be preferable if they did not," Mr. Nettleton remarked.

"You understand, William, that we have not questioned your sincerity, nor have we lost interest in your noble work," the Rev. Mr. Savage assured him.

"I accept your assurance," William said stiffly.

William left the meeting in a despondent mood. In his eagerness to do what he felt to be the will of the Lord he had not thought for a moment that his efforts would be rebuffed by earnest Christians. He expected that the devil — and for him Satan was a real person — would seek to impede his work. It could be assumed that Beelzebub would inspire toughs to pelt him with overripe eggs and create disturbances at his street meetings, but he had not thought that fellow Christians would fail him.

But finally the humor of the situation overwhelmed him and he began to laugh, chortling until the tears ran down his cheeks. He had become so accustomed to the odors of street crowds — and, after all, they were not so pungent in the out-of-doors as they were inside a chapel—that he had not even noticed them in the sanctuary of Wesley Chapel. Beyond a doubt his eager congregation from the street did have noticeable odors. He wouldn't make that mistake again.

But, if this had been a setback to his youthful enthusiasm, he did not allow it to be a permanent handicap. The next evening he was back on the street once more, preaching with all his heart and soul to a slum crowd in Nottingham.

He was working at the time as a pawnbroker's assistant, a job which he despised, but one that his father esteemed most highly since Samuel Booth, in William's own words, "knew no greater gain nor end than money."

William's father had been a man of some considerable means and he had as his goal the training of his children to be "ladies and gentlemen." That meant that they had to be enrolled in the right schools and that they should be prepared to enter a life of leisure and luxury. Unfortunately, he was a poor businessman and lost everything that he possessed in wild speculation.

His children had to be taken out of school, and William had been apprenticed to a pawnbroker to learn what Samuel Booth considered a business which would be bound to bring young William to the top financially.

Samuel Booth can best be described as an altogether conventional individual. He could not think of doing anything out of the ordinary. He was Wesleyan in his church affiliation because by the middle of the nineteenth century Methodists were good, substantial, middle class people. But William had no religious training whatsoever in his home. The Booths did not even have grace before meals in their household.

The sole religious instruction which William received from his mother consisted of the injunction, "Be good, William, and all will be well." But to "be good" meant basically, "Be respectable." It meant that people who aspired to be ladies and gentlemen refrained from doing anything unconventional. It was a negative kind of morality upon which the boy was being nurtured, and it didn't satisfy his eager, sensitive soul.

William's first glimpse of the meaning of faith came from one of his cousins, a shoemaker whose name was Gregory. As Gregory was working one day at his bench he spoke to the tall lad who was watching him with interest and said, "Willie Booth, do you know that religion is something that comes to you from outside of you?" William later told his minister, a tall, dark-haired contemplative individual, Parson Wyatt, what his cousin had said but the parson's only comment had been delivered in a pious tone of voice, "William, you will soon be teaching in the Sunday school."

Street preaching is altogether different from proclaiming the Gospel in the respectable environs of a church or cathedral. William was often greeted with a barrage of overripe fruits and vegetables when he stood on a street corner, earnestly pouring out his heart to whatever crowd would gather. Drunken men and women and callow youths cursed and jeered at him. But his sturdiest adversary in Nottingham was a character known as "Besom Jack." The man seldom drew a sober breath. His sole means of livelihood was the sale of brooms from door to door, but he spent all of his earnings on drink.

Neighbors frequently called upon the constables to take him into custody when he beat his wife with more than customary ferocity. She was a poor slattern who for years had put up with his evil ways without murmuring. She was forced to beg crusts of bread and used tea leaves in order to have the most meager meals on her table. However, coupled with Jack's vile temper was a sense of humor of sorts. He took particular delight in disturbing the young preacher, challenging William's statements, jeering at him in the middle of a sermon, and aiding and abetting urchins who pelted William with rocks and rotten eggs.

William never lost his temper although he would point out in bold language the ultimate destiny in eternity of those who would not listen to the preaching of the Word. He was willing to suffer any personal affront himself and thought little of it. But he felt that those who ill treated one who spoke in the name of and for God were in danger of hell-fire, and he did not hesitate to call their attention to what he conceived would be their ultimate fate.

After imbibing copiously of stout, Besom Jack would tipsily seek out the street corner where William would be holding forth.

"Thinks he's a preacher, Skinny does," he would shout, "but did you ever hear such drivel as wot 'e spouts? Dry up, Long Shanks! Dry up!"

A roar of laughter would come from the crowd although some few would urge Jack to be quiet.

"Quiet? W'y should I be? Ain't I got as much right to spout as yon skinny-legs? Come off y'r perch, lad, and let a man preach as 'as got summat to siy!"

William had a resounding voice and could usually drown out the man's jibes but he still found it difficult to preach under such unfavorable circumstances. Nevertheless, he persisted in proclaiming his message.

One night, however, after he had dismissed the crowd he fell in with Besom Jack and walked along with him.

"Why do you do it?" he asked the man. "Why persist in interrupting one who is seeking to proclaim a message from God? These people need salvation but you are their stumbling block. If you will not let God come into your own life, why withhold Him from others?"

"Anyone who wills to do so is free to go forrud," Besom Jack countered.

"But you make it difficult, if not well-nigh impossible for them to do so," William asserted.

"I was not intendin' to do that," Jack replied soberly.

"That is what you do, ne'ertheless," William reminded him.

"For that I'm truly sorry, maan," Besom Jack asserted. " 'Twas not my desire to do so."

"Would you be willing, then, to kneel down here and now and tell God you're sorry?" William urged. "It matters not if you do ill to me. It matters much that you have done ill to God."

"I've never prayed in me whole life before," Jack protested.

"Then, 'twould be a good time to begin now."

"I'll think on it."

"Shall we stop here and wait until you've finished thinking?" William asked. "It should not take you long to come to a decision."

But Besom Jack was canny.

"No, maan, not now. Let me think on it in me lodgin's."

"Very well, but don't put it off. Think on it tonight and tomorrow at the meeting tell me about it, and we can pray together."

"I'm not any hand at prayin', I told ye."

"But you're a great hand at talking," William replied.

"Oh, aye."

"Well, praying is just talking. All you need to do is talk to God, telling him you're sorry."

"I'll think on it."

Besom Jack was not back on the corner where William preached the next evening. William felt both relieved and unhappy, relieved because Besom Jack was not present to stir up the crowd, unhappy because he felt that Jack had been close to a decision and somehow William felt that he was responsible because Jack had not come through.

Nor was Jack there the following evening. William would have sought for him but he had no idea where the man lived. Nightly he scanned the crowd, but evidently Jack was not going to return to the meetings.

William prayed for him, earnestly and patiently on his knees, the last thing before he retired at night, the first thing when he arose in the morning, bringing the man and his needs before the throne of grace by name. Nightly also he prayed for him on the street corner, but these prayers did not mention the name of the one for whom they were offered. Instead, William asked God's special blessing upon one who was near to decision, that he might be led to make his choice; but he did not parade the name of Besom Jack for the crowd to hear.

A week went by, then two weeks. By day and night prayers

were offered up for Besom Jack, but he did not put in an appearance.

One evening as William began to preach he was interrupted by raucous calls from a crowd of young toughs who were assembled on the outskirts of the group. William raised his voice so that it might be heard above the commotion which they were creating.

Suddenly there was a loud shout from someone on the fringe of the crowd.

"Stop it, stop it, I say," the voice shouted. "Give the young preacher a chance! He's sayin' words you should hear, words I want to listen to, the worst sinner, I."

It was the familiar voice of Besom Jack.

William stopped short. All eyes turned in Jack's direction. The youths who had been shouting were quiet. For a moment there was no sound except the clop-clop of horses' hooves as gentlefolk drove by in their fine carriages.

Finally William spoke.

"Besom Jack!" he said quietly but in tones that penetrated to the far corner of the crowd. "Have you reached a decision, man?"

"Aye!" Besom Jack shouted joyfully. "That I have. If the Lord will have me I'm fer Him."

"Come forward then," William exclaimed. "Come forward and we'll have our prayer."

Besom Jack made his way through the crowd.

"Jack and I will kneel in prayer," William announced, "and as many of you as will join us can also kneel."

Jack and William knelt on the rough cobblestones. They were hard on William's bony knees but he took no notice of discomfort. The Lord had laid His hand upon the heart of a recalcitrant sinner. Physical discomfort meant nothing to him although his chest would be constricted the morning after from the chill, and his knees would be stiff.

All about him others began to kneel.

William poured out his heart to God, asking the Eternal to save the soul of Besom Jack, to help him break the grip of alcohol upon his body, and to give him the grace and power to witness to His holy Name. Others joined in the petition. "Hallelujahs" and "Praise God's" resounded up and down the street.

Others were caught up as in a tidal wave of emotion. Even the young hoodlums were quiet. Finally several of them came

18

forward and whispered to William that they would like to have him pray for them. Older people joined the company of those around Besom Jack.

William realized that he had in that company the nucleus for a church, but there was no building where they could meet and he was not a minister of the Gospel. He sensed that something more was needed than he had to offer.

Therefore, when young and old had made their confessions of faith, William arose from his knees and quietly said, "This has been a wonderful experience both for you and me. But it is not enough. Go to church next Sunday and tell the minister what you have decided here tonight. Join the church and make your testimony for righteousness and clean living and salvation. It isn't enough to say that you stand for Christ. Join other Christians that you may make your profession count. Christ established the Church. Go, and link yourselves to His Church and then become busy for the Lord."

CHAPTER 2

William Booth found himself in a grave quandry. He was a loyal member of Wesley Chapel which was, as has been indicated, a stronghold of middle class Methodist orthodoxy. The church had strongly influenced young William in his thinking.

True Methodist fervor was constantly in evidence within its walls. Sunday afternoons there were Love Feasts where men and women testified freely of their religious experiences. The senior minister of the church was the Rev. Samuel Dunn, superintendent of the circuit of which Wesley Chapel was the principal preaching point.

A so-called circuit in Methodism in the British Isles consisted of several chapels which were banded together into a single entity, similar to the collegiate churches of the Dutch Reformed faith in America, of which the Marble Collegiate Church in New York City is an excellent example.

The superintendent of the circuit was the senior minister of the group and he had several ordained ministers and a number of lay workers serving under him. The Rev. Mr. Dunn was a man of considerable learning but cold, obstinate and autocratic.

In later years William Booth always spoke gratefully of his influence, but it was basically the influence of an army sergeant,
ruling with an iron hand the soldiers in his squad, and not the
kindly encouragement of love and understanding.

William respected Dr. Dunn despite the latter's coldness,
and he accepted frequent rebuffs from him without complaint.
He belonged to a Bible class led by an elderly man who was
also custodian of the chapel, a genial, chubby character named
Sammy Statham.

When Dr. Dunn wanted a young man to do some village
preaching for him Statham told him that he knew just the man
to qualify for the assignment, and summoned William to confer
with the minister.

"Can you preach?" Dr. Dunn inquired.

"I've been preaching in the streets now for some months,"
William replied confidently. "I'm sure that I could preach acceptable sermons in villages."

"And by whose authority did you begin your preaching?"
Dr. Dunn inquired coldly. "Have I given you leave?"

William hung his head and acknowledged that he had
never even thought to ask for permission. He expected a rebuke
but Dr. Dunn merely remarked, " 'Twould have been better,
Will, to have requested permission but, although you failed to
do so I certainly would not forbid you."

"Then do I have your permission to continue?"

"Indeed yes, but don't undertake other labors of this sort
without securing authority to engage in them."

William promised to abide by this dictum.

Several months later Dr. Dunn summoned William to meet
him in his study.

"Since our last conference," he remarked, "I have heard
many good reports of your labors, William; and I have followed
your work with considerable interest."

"Truly, they have not been my labors, Dr. Dunn," William
replied. "If some success has attended my preaching it is due
to the fact that the Lord has been able to use me and not to
any ability on my part."

"Of course, of course," the doctor agreed dryly, "but still
we must realize that you have been willing to have the Lord
use you. I shall come right to the point, lad. Our work in the
chapel and in our other halls is growing so rapidly that we could
use another minister, and it occurred to me that you would be
the one for the position.

"To be sure," he added, "you would not be called upon to preach in Wesley Chapel but we could use you in the out stations. You are over young for such labors but that is a fault which time will remedy."

Dr. Dunn vouchsafed a vinegary smile.

"But I am otherwise employed," William replied. "My preaching heretofore has all been in addition to my regular work. And I need the wages that I receive to help my mother at home. She has a little shop but her income from it is not sufficient to maintain our family."

"If you are more engrossed with the things of this world . . ." Dr. Dunn essayed.

"But assuredly I am not," William replied. "I can think of no employment more detestable than that of a pawnbroker save the vocation of a publican. But my father apprenticed me to that work and it is the only thing I know. God helping me, some day I shall be able to devote full time to the Lord, but I am now only able to give my evenings to preaching His blessed word."

Dr. Dunn warmed considerably.

"I can see that you have your problem, William," he agreed, "but some day you must enter completely into the Lord's service. I know few young men who are so well endowed for preaching as you are."

"Thank you, sir," William humbly replied.

Despite the man's frigidity and autocratic ways it is quite probable that Dr. Dunn influenced William more than anyone aside from an American evangelist, a Rev. Dr. Caughey, and a Mr. Isaac Marsden. The latter is scarcely ever mentioned in William's writings but when he is it is always with a reverence and respect that indicate the influence he had on the growing lad.

Early in his teens, shortly after his father's death and the discovery that Samuel Booth was virtually bankrupt, William also became interested in politics. The Chartists of that period were literally the Labor Party of the era, and an impassioned Irishman, Feargus O'Connor, made a deep impression upon the lad.

O'Connor was a fiery orator with none of the unctuous ways of the smooth politician. As champion of the underdog, pleading the cause of the working man, he appealed to young William. If it had not been for William's growing conviction that politics were not enough, that it was not sufficient to change an environment in which people lived but that the hearts of those people also had to be changed, William might have become a great reforming politician.

An echo of William's feeling was heard in World War II when Leslie Weatherhead, probably the most influential preacher in London in his generation, commenting on the destruction of the slum area by German aircraft, remarked that this was regarded by many as a blessing but the destruction of physical slums was not sufficient: As long as there were slums in people's hearts, England would have a slum problem.

William Booth would not have expressed these sentiments in the same words but this was how he felt. People were living in sin and degradation. He wanted to save their souls but he sensed that there was also a great need for them to be saved from filth and poverty. And in these formative years were born some of the principles which later became cardinal tenets of the Salvation Army.

In 1848, when he was nineteen years of age, William's apprenticeship came to an end. He was glad to be free of the bondage of a pawnbroker's office but it was the only work he knew. Consequently he joined the large army of the unemployed.

Daily he walked the streets of Nottingham, seeking employment, but none was to be had. Although discouraged, he would come home with a cheery smile.

"The Lord will open the way for me," he would tell his mother.

The fact that he was jobless gave him greater sympathy for those who listened to him preach, many of them also lacking employment.

One night a young tough shouted at him, "It's easy enough for you toffs to come a-slummin' down here, but what do you know about how we-uns feel — no jobs, no nothin'?"

William fixed the young man with a piercing gaze.

"I'm not a toff," he said. "I've been wearing out shoe leather for months now, trying to find honest employment. My mother keeps a little shop. My father is dead. And I'll take any kind of work — as long as it's honest."

The young man hung his head.

"I'm sorry," he mumbled. "I didn't know."

It was a wonderful opening for the young evangelist.

"The only thing I have which you are lacking is the saving knowledge of Jesus Christ," William said. "Christ was a working man like you and me. He understood our problems. He knew what it meant to go hungry at times. And He has saved me from my sins and is ready and willing to save you also. You can look for a job with your head up and chin out if you will take Him for your Saviour, believe on Him, and trust Him to walk beside you."

"I'll take Him," the young man shouted. "I always thought He was the God of the rich, but if He's int'rested in the likes of me I'll believe on Him."

"Glory, Hallelujah!" William shouted.

Throughout the period of his unemployment William continued to preach every night, and daily to look for a job. In every spare moment, realizing his need for greater knowledge of the workings of Providence, he read Finney's *Sermons and Lectures,* and studied the works of Whitefield and Wesley. He probably would have become discouraged if, while seeking employment, he had not had his other work to do — preaching nightly, praying in cottages, attending services on Sundays in the chapels.

Finally he decided, after almost twelve months of unemployment, that he would never be able to secure remunerative work in Nottingham and, with empty pockets, he started out for London.

The London of 1849 was in the throes of the beginnings of the machine age. Science was becoming a watchword. Railroads were just beginning to throw their ribbons of steel across the island.

The condition of the poor beggared description. There was no system of national education. Children were permitted to work in factories and on the docks for ten hours a day before they had even come into their teens. Charles Dickens was calling attention through his novels to the wretched lot of multitudes but there was no such thing as a social conscience.

And the religion of Jesus Christ was regarded as the exclusive prerogative of the well-to-do and the middle class. In a sense it was almost considered a luxury. It was assumed that God was on the side of the privileged, rewarding those who did not violate — openly, at least — the Ten Commandments which had been given at Sinai.

In later years, when he was writing his own autobiography, William headed one chapter, "London." In a single word he summed up his impression of the city. It was "Loneliness." He was friendless, jobless and homesick.

He had one anchor in London, his sister Ann, the beautiful

young woman, older than he, whom he regarded as an angel. He was certain that her home would be a haven for him. Ann had married one of William's boyhood friends whom he also considered quite near to perfection. But upon arriving in London the man had become imbued with a desire to make his fortune speedily. He had cut corners in business, had become an agnostic and a thoroughgoing materialist. Coupled with these characteristics was an incipient alcoholism.

Ann herself had changed and become much like her husband. She still loved her brother but was too much afraid of her husband to take William's part when the husband treated him with ill-concealed contempt. William's sister and her husband were deteriorating so rapidly in both morals and their material welfare that within a short time after William reached London they were completely impoverished and died soon afterwards.

Aside from preaching, William knew only one business, that of pawnbroking. Finally, to keep from starving, he secured a position in a loan shop in Walworth. The man for whom he worked was nominally a Christian but smugly considered religion as the adoption of a series of tenets which blessed a man who refrained from certain low vices but which had little to do with his relations to his fellow men.

William was even more restricted as to time than he had been in Nottingham. He was only allowed time off on the Sabbath and one additional hour one day a week. He performed his duties faithfully in the shop but longed for the opportunity to preach. Perhaps the fact that his time was so limited created the deeper yearning for the vocation to which he could give himself heart and soul.

At about this time Wesleyan Methodism was in the throes of revolution. It should be recalled that John Wesley, differing from Knox and Calvin, had had no plan for the government of a Methodist Church. One section of Wesleyan Methodism was eager to give greater power to the conference, tending toward an episcopate, the other believed that the churches themselves should be autonomous, akin to Congregationalism.

Strangely enough, at this time William felt that the welfare of the church demanded a strong authoritarianism and he cast in his lot with the Connexionalists. As with most church controversies, tempers flared and charges and countercharges flew back and forth. Despite his youth William's advice was eagerly sought and both sides attempted to win him to their point of view. William's preaching had nothing to do with the controversy and, because he did not take sides, extremists in both camps felt that his voice and presence were needed in their support.

A shrewd businessman, a Mr. E. H. Rabbits, a boot manufacturer, was especially eager to secure William's allegiance. He belonged to the Reformers who insisted that each individual chapel should be an entity in itself. Methodist groups, it will be recalled, were not regarded as churches but were still considered societies. Loyal Wesleyans regarded themselves as members of the Anglican Church but were so far weaned away from it that they only attended the Methodist chapels.

In June, 1851, Mr. Rabbits persuaded William to work with the Reformers, holding out to him the hope that William would soon be able to spend all of his time in preaching and could enter the ministry.

Later still, in the spring of 1852, Mr. Rabbits came to him with a proposal that he give up his job and spend full time in preaching.

"That's impossible," William informed him. "Who would want me? I'm too young to serve as the pastor of a church. Street preaching, yes. I have done much of that and it has been with a measure of success, but to undertake to be the pastor of a church, that's different."

Mr. Rabbits eyed him shrewdly.

"You're probably right about a ministry in the church. But I'm talking about evangelism. You could conduct a revival service in a chapel and be as successful as you have been in street evangelism."

"But the churches couldn't support me in this endeavor," William replied. "I must have a job in order to eat. I can't live on air."

Mr. Rabbits laughed.

"That's true," he replied, "and I suspect that it takes a sight of groceries to keep that big frame of yours alive. But how much would you need?"

William began to add up the costs in his own mind. He would be able to do his own cooking and would not need to dine out. He could launder his own shirts, albeit he recognized that ironing them might be somewhat difficult.

After careful calculation he came up with a figure.

"I don't think that I could get along on less than twelve shillings a week," he said.

"Nonsense!" Mr. Rabbits retorted. "You couldn't possibly make it. You'd be begging in a fortnight. You'd need at least twenty."

"Never that!" William replied. "But I know I can subsist on twelve shillings."

"Impossible!" Mr. Rabbits asserted positively.

Williams shrugged his shoulders.

"Have it your own way," he said, "but where would I get twelve shillings — let alone twenty?"

"I'll underwrite you for twenty a week," Mr. Rabbits promised, adding cautiously, "at least for the first three months. By that time your collections will probably take care of your needs."

William pondered the proposal. There was security in his work in the pawnshop. If he left his job it would be doubtful if he could return to it at the end of the three months' period should his work as an evangelist not prove successful. But he hesitated for only a moment.

"I'll take it, Mr. Rabbits," William agreed, "trusting in God that this undertaking is in accord with His will."

"I'm confident that the Lord will bless your labors."

But William's employer was exceedingly unhappy. William's services had been secured for a pittance and he had been most conscientious and, his employer was aware, unlike other young men whom he had engaged, William's hand had never dipped into the till.

"If you needed more money why didn't you let me know?" he grumbled. "I would gladly have raised your salary. You had better reconsider your decision."

"It isn't a matter of money," William replied. "I want to spend my life proclaiming my Saviour to a lost world."

"But it has cost me money to train you," the man wailed, "and just when you were beginning to earn what I have been paying you, you up and leave."

"I had had my training in the business before ever I worked for you," William reminded him.

"Just the same it's rank folly," the man asserted.

"It isn't folly to do my Master's will," William returned.

"Don't ever expect to come back here," was the retort. "You'll be through in a few months but I'll not take you back even though you drag your tail like a whipped cur."

With those words ringing in his ears William set forth. He had been living in an attic over the shop and so, as he began new work, he had to find lodgings. He located a room in the home of an elderly widow and was able to rent it for five shillings a week. He went to a furniture store where he purchased some chairs and other articles of furniture.

The next day was Good Friday, April 10, 1852. In his own autobiography, written some years later, he described the events of this memorable day as follows:

"Three things marked the day that followed the one on which I shook hands with my cold-hearted master and said 'good-bye.' One of these proved of no little importance, both to myself and to the world at large, in the years that followed.

1. The first day of my freedom was Good Friday.

2. It was also my birthday, the tenth of April.

3. The third, and most important of all, was that on that day I fell over head and ears in love with the precious woman who afterwards became my wife."

CHAPTER 3

William had acquired a superb self-confidence when it came to street preaching. There was always a challenge confronting him as he took his place on a busy corner. Young hoodlums constantly interrupted him. An occasional atheist or agnostic would challenge some statement that he made. In essence street preaching inevitably presented a conflict.

Preaching in a chapel was altogether different. It also presented a challenge, but one of a different nature. There were no cat-calls, no shouting, and no carts rumbled by as he gave his messages.

But on the night that William began his evangelistic meeting indoors he encountered a much more potent distraction than the yells of ragamuffins, for William fell in love. The object of his affection was a Miss Catherine Mumford who lived in Brixton, at that time a picturesque suburb of London where many people of influence were living. Catherine was the only daughter in the family but she had four brothers. She had been brought up puritanically but lovingly. Both her mother and father were strong-minded individuals and Catherine inherited their forcefulness, but she had particular qualities of her own.

Not a stray dog nor a bird with a broken leg but Catherine befriended it. At times the home in Brixton took on the aspect of a pet hospital, and she was quite likely, even as a small child, to bring home some drunken derelict for luncheon or dinner.

Mr. Rabbits had asked William to preach that evening at a service of the Reformers in a school room situated in Cowper Street, City Road. William and Catherine had actually met before but on this particular evening, when William saw her in the congregation, he fell deeply in love. William was always one to believe in direct action and the service was no sooner concluded than he made his way unostentatiously to her side. He was stopped several times en route by people who wished to congratulate him on his message but he kept his eyes on Catherine and finally reached her side.

Remembering their previous meeting, William spoke to her immediately.

"Miss Mumford," he said, "I am William Booth."

Her dimples flashed.

"So I assumed," she remarked innocently, "especially since Mr. Rabbits informed us that that was your name."

"But I met you before in his home," he protested.

"I remember the occasion," she agreed.

"I am glad that you do," he asserted, adding boldly, "and I would like very much to accompany you to your home."

"I should be delighted to have the pleasure of your company," she said demurely, her eyes downcast.

Later on they could not remember what they discussed except that they revealed to one another their inmost thoughts and desires. It was almost eleven o'clock when they reached Brixton, an unheard of hour in that generation for a young man and woman to be sauntering along the streets.

Mrs. Mumford was waiting up for Catherine. Evidently she had worried about her daughter but, if she did, she gave no sign of it except for a sigh of relief that her daughter had arrived home safe and sound.

"Since it is quite late could you not abide with us tonight?" Mrs. Mumford suggested to William. "We have a spare room and would be delighted if you could stay and then breakfast with us in the morning."

"But it will surely inconvenience you," William replied halfheartedly.

"Not in the least," Mrs. Mumford replied.

28

"It would be particularly appropriate to have William stay here since this is his birthday," Catherine added.

"Your birthday!" Mrs. Mumford exclaimed. "We should have celebrated by having a party."

"Perhaps we could tomorrow," Catherine suggested.

"Oh, no," William protested.

"How old are you, William?" Mrs. Mumford inquired.

"Twenty-three today, Ma'am," William replied.

"Exceedingly young to be a preacher," Mrs. Mumford exclaimed.

"Oh, but I couldn't truly be called a preacher," William protested. "At least, I have never had the necessary education for the pulpit. But I have been speaking on street corners, proclaiming the Gospel, ever since I was sixteen. I am actually considered an evangelist, and I hope to make that my vocation for life."

"Isn't it wonderful, Mother?" Catherine exclaimed, her eyes shining.

"Truly it is," her mother replied. "But have you been preaching in chapels for some time?"

"Tonight was my first such experience," William acknowledged.

"But how did you become acquainted with Catherine?" Mrs. Mumford inquired.

"I met her once before at the home of Mr. Rabbits," William replied.

"Only once before?" Mrs. Mumford asked.

"Only once," William assured her.

"And then you asked if you could see her home this evening?"

"Yes."

"Why?"

The unexpectedness and directness of the question took William unawares. For a moment he was tempted to vouchsafe a specious reply, but he believed so sincerely that one must at all times tell the truth, albeit to do so might prove embarrassing, that he felt he had to make a completely honest reply. Although he had been thus far unacquainted with the symptoms of love he knew that he had asked Miss Mumford for the privilege of escorting her home because he had fallen deeply in love with her, and, if there had been any question about his feeling before they had walked along together, there was none when they arrived at Catherine's home.

Hence he blurted out bluntly, "Mrs. Mumford, this may sound altogether strange to you but I found myself falling in love with your daughter this evening. I felt that I *had* to converse with her. I have no doubt that we walked too slowly. I hope that you will pardon me for keeping her out for such a long time; and I hope that you will forgive this bold statement but it's true. And, Catherine, I trust that you, too, will forgive me."

Catherine's face was scarlet but she said shyly, "Truly, William, there is nothing to forgive."

"Definitely not," Mrs. Mumford agreed, "but I should like to know, Mr. Booth, just what your intentions are. Catherine has already had one unfortunate experience, and I do not want my daughter to pass through another such ordeal again."

"My intentions!" William inquired blankly.

"Yes, your intentions," Mrs. Mumford flatly insisted. "Are you interested in breaking young women's hearts, adding Catherine to a list of conquests, or do you intend to marry her?"

William's face flamed brick red.

"I can assure you, Mrs. Mumford, that I have no list of conquests. I have never fallen in love before, never even walked home with a young lady from chapel or any other meeting."

"But are you concerned about marriage, or do you just want to dawdle along with my daughter?" pursued Mrs. Mumford directly.

"I wish that we could be married at once," William blurted out, "but I have only a few shillings to my name and only three months' assured salary as an evangelist. And in my work I don't suppose that I'll ever be settled in one place — for some years, at least. I had not given any thought to marriage but I suspect that it is out of the question for some years to come."

"Why, then, did you single out Catherine for your intentions?" pursued Mrs. Mumford gently but grimly.

"Merely to converse with her, merely for companionship," William replied.

"Mother, I can assure you that there was nothing romantic in our conversation or conduct tonight," Catherine protested. "I like William, and evidently he likes me or he would not have sought my company this evening, but we have no thought of marriage."

William had to confess to himself that Catherine didn't altogether express his own feelings but decided not to take issue with her.

Mrs. Mumford continued.

"Inevitably, my dear," she said, "an attachment of this kind ripens — or should be allowed to ripen — into love."

"I'm sorry, indeed," William said, "that our innocent conversation has been so greatly misconstrued. I think I had best be leaving."

He picked up his hat and made for the door, dismissing all thought of occupying the spare room for the night, and breakfasting with the family — and with Catherine especially — in the morning.

"Good night, William," Catherine murmured.

"Good night, Catherine," William returned. Turning to Mrs. Mumford he remarked politely, "And I bid you good evening, Ma'am."

"Good night, Mr. Booth," she said.

William set out for his lodgings, a prey to various emotions. He knew without a doubt that Catherine was the one person in all the world for him. He was positive that he wanted to marry her; but how could he do it, his prospects being what they were? And the Mumfords' standing in the world was quite evidently such that it would be difficult for their daughter to accept the scale of living to which he was accustomed.

What should he do? Having met and fallen in love with her, should he now give up all thought of her? Should he put her completely out of his mind?

William knew the answer. He definitely should forget her for her own good; but he also knew that she was the one person in the world with whom his life could be linked for service to Christ. Only a woman with such a warm heart and such a personal passion for the Saviour would be able to be his helpmeet in the ministry of Christ.

He knew that he could not give her up. Never, if he lived to be as old as Methusaleh, could he forget her. As he walked along to his home that evening plans kept flashing through his mind. He would try to get a church and settle down to married life.

Yet he felt unsuited to the pastoral experience, and he was also unprepared for it. His bent was toward evangelistic preaching. As well try to make a silk purse of a sow's ear as to make a settled preacher of him! But the evangelistic program of the Reformers was no life to share with a young wife. Even less was it the life that a growing family should live, and he realized that he could not marry Catherine unless he was also willing to have a family.

There was but one thing to do — forget Catherine.

This was the decision which he made before he reached his lodgings. It was the only sensible thing to do. As they had walked along that evening Catherine had confided to him that her health was precarious. She had frequent periods of illness. If he were to marry he should have a sturdy wife. But he could not conceive of marrying anyone but her.

There was one other factor to consider. The career on which he was embarking was not clearly defined. Mr. Rabbits was willing to pay him three months' salary but there were no engagements arranged beforehand. He had no idea where his meetings would be held.

Within a few days, however, the situation changed. The little congregation to which he preached invited him to serve as pastor. Thus it happened that he found himself serving the small company of Reformers which Catherine had joined, becoming, in effect, her pastor.

It was a delightful arrangement for William but it was not one which offered him a sufficient living even for himself and certainly not one which would maintain a young couple.

But William began living in a world consisting of roseate clouds. He could see Catherine frequently. Yet the more he saw of her the farther away seemed the consummation of his dreams. He had to marry Catherine — but he couldn't. He wouldn't marry her under the circumstances but he continued to hope that something would happen which would make it possible for them to be united in matrimony.

A few evenings after he had accepted the appointment he dropped in at the Mumford home for a talk with her regarding his feelings and his prospects.

"I can't ask you to marry me, dearest," he admitted, "and yet I can think of nothing but marriage with you. I know it's impractical: I know I don't earn enough to make it possible for us to establish a home, but I feel that life would be empty without you at my side."

"I feel the same way, William," Catherine acknowledged. "And since we have reached a point where we cannot find a solution to our problem by ourselves I would suggest that we place it before the Almighty. I am confident that He can help us."

"A capital plan," William agreed. "Let's pray together now."

The two knelt and clasped hands and told the Father what their hopes and aspirations were. They ended their prayer by committing their ways to Him and agreeing to follow His will.

Having done so they arose and William seized her in a great bear hug. He was about to give her an affectionate kiss but Catherine pushed him away.

"Such familiarities would be altogether wrong," she protested, "until we are able to announce to the world that we will be married and are ready to name the date for the nuptials."

"You mean that such an innocent expression of affection as a kiss is out of . . ." William began.

"I mean that we must refrain from every appearance of evil," she explained.

"Well, such stiff-necked . . ." William exploded.

"If you are unwilling to abide . . ." Catherine retorted.

"Oh, I'll go along with you," he agreed, "but I must say that I consider it altogether prudish and . . ."

"If you desire to break . . ."

"No, no," he hastened to say. "I'll accept it."

However, he did so unwillingly. He could see nothing wrong with loving demonstrations of affection between two earnest Christian people intent on matrimony. Still, if Catherine insisted. . . .

That night, in the quiet of his own room, William sought guidance in an old familiar rite. He was confident that God would speak to him if he would open a Bible, with his eyes closed, place a finger on the first passage it encountered, then open his eyes and read. He was often told by Catherine and others that this was practically a heathen method of seeking divine guidance, but he stoutly maintained that it was a practical way of letting God speak to him.

Thus, that evening, he followed his customary practice.

He blew out his candle after first placing his Bible within easy reach. Then he stretched out his hand for the book, opened it, and placed his long finger on a passage. With his other hand he struck a match and relit the candle.

Carefully he read the passage at which his finger was pointing.

The verse which he had thus indicated read: "And the two sticks became one in my hand."

For William it was as if the voice of God had spoken to him. He needed no further word to confirm his belief that Catherine was intended by God to be his spouse and that in God's own time He would bring the nuptials to pass.

William was so busy for the next few days that he could

not see Catherine but finally, after a lapse of four days which seemed like four years, he visited her and told her what the Scriptures had revealed to him.

"You don't take such an omen seriously?" she asked. "That is well-nigh witchcraft."

"I disagree," William replied. "For me it was the voice of God."

He was so earnest that Catherine could not find the heart to chide him more.

"You are so sincere, William, that even though I can't feel that it is thus that the Spirit speaks to the heart of man, perhaps He has done so this time," Catherine told him. "All I can say is that I am content to wait until we can be married. If we are unable to set aside sufficient funds within the next few years for our nuptials, still I shall wait a lifetime for you. If we are never able to consummate our marriage I shall go to the grave unwed. You are the only one I love. You will always be my only, my dearest, love."

"Catherine, my darling," William murmured, but made no move to embrace her.

Seemingly of a joint volition, however, the two knelt side by side and plighted their troth. In the correspondence which followed it was indicated that, although they had no intention of consummating a marriage out of wedlock, they did consider themselves bound eternally by the promises which each had made.

If the course of true love began to run smoothly for William the course of his service in the ministry did not. Although he was gladly received at the outset, after he began his work the leaders in the chapel began to treat him with pronounced coldness. They refused to give him any authority as a minister and the opportunities to preach became fewer and fewer.

Finally William and Catherine faced the situation together.

"If the Wesleyans will not have you why don't you go to the Congregationalists, dear?" she suggested.

"But they are predestinarian," William objected. The tone of his voice indicated that for him predestination was closely akin to atheism.

"Have you ever heard the doctrine preached in a Congregational church?" Catherine inquired.

"No."

"Or, for that matter, have you ever heard a Presbyterian preach on the subject? They are reputed to cling more tena-

34

ciously to the doctrine than even the Congregationalists do," she remarked.

"No, I have never heard a Presbyterian minister speak on the subject."

"Well, then, perhaps they no longer adhere to it," Catherine suggested.

"But if it is a part of their book of common worship — or whatever they call it — it would appear that I had accepted it if I were ordained by them," William countered.

"But if they don't preach on the subject surely you wouldn't be expected to do so," she argued.

"I'll call on Dr. Campbell. He is the editor of their church newspaper," William announced decisively.

The next day he paid a visit to Dr. Campbell and made an excellent impression on him. Although Dr. Campbell dearly loved a theological controversy and his magazine, *The British Banner*, rarely published an issue in which Dr. Campbell did not fulminate against those who did not see eye to eye with him, he was essentially a warmhearted individual and especially kind to those who seemed on the verge of renouncing views which he regarded as unorthodox.

But William did not want to become a Congregationalist by coming into the church under false colors, and for that reason he asked the cleric some exceedingly searching questions.

"Would I be expected to preach any other doctrine than the universal love of God?" was the first question which he propounded.

"Not at all," the doctor replied. "As a minister you would not be expected to espouse anything which you did not honestly believe."

Dr. Campbell added, "To be sure, since your education up to this point has been so limited — through no fault of your own, of course — you will have to go to college and learn there how to study your Bible. What you find in it you must go out and preach, and that will be all that Independents would ask of you."

During the course of their conference other ministers joined them and they substantiated what Dr. Campbell told him.

A week later he met with the committee appointed to examine him for admission to the training institute. Chairman of this committee was Dr. George Smith.

"We understand that you have been reared among the Wesleyans," Dr. Smith vouchsafed. "They are an earnest people and undoubtedly sincere, but their theology is decidedly at variance with our own. You understand that, because Dr. Campbell has so earnestly commended you, we are inclined to overlook certain . . . shall we say . . . deviations from Congregational orthodoxy. We are showing you special favor in arranging for you to go into training although you are not a member of a Congregational church and hold doctrinal views at variance with our own.

"It is only fair to advise you that at the close of the first term the committee will certainly expect you to espouse theological views more in accord with those which are held by the committee."

Another member jumped to his feet.

"Dr. Smith," he exclaimed, "would it not be in order to suggest to the young man that he begin his preparation by studying Booth's *Reign of Grace* and Payne's *Divine Sovereignty?* These two magnificent tomes would do much to set the lad on the right track."

"An excellent suggestion, indeed," Dr. Smith replied. "Excellent. You would do well to accept this advice," he added, turning to William.

Earnestly William responded.

"I shall be most happy to do so," he assured them.

On his way home William stopped at a bookseller's to purchase the volumes which had been recommended. Arriving at his quarters, he immediately set about the task of digesting the books. He read thirty or forty pages of *Reign of Grace* and then threw the book down.

William needed the opportunity to preach which the Independents offered him. He wanted very much to take the courses which would prepare him for the ministry, but he read enough to know that he could never accept the doctrines of the Independents. He took up a pen and put down on paper the reasons why he could not go to the training school.

But now he was faced with the difficult problem of making a living. He could go back to pawnbroking but his soul rebelled at the idea. Yet he had given away his last sixpence. William Booth was frequently guilty of doing that through all the years of his life. If someone was in need — and on this occasion it was a tubercular young woman who lacked food — his warm heart dictated to an almost vacant purse that it should empty itself completely to succor the hungry or desolate.

William had just about decided that two denominational groups had turned their backs completely upon him when friends among the Reformers found a place for him in a community in the south of Lincolnshire. Someone was needed to ride a circuit with its central point in Spalding and a number of outlying preaching points.

As soon as William received the invitation to undertake the assignment he hurried over to the Mumford's.

"We have it, Catherine. We have it," he exclaimed exultingly.

"We have what, William? Sit down and catch your breath and then tell me what we have that is so important."

William dropped into a chair.

"We have God's answer to our problem," he said. "They've asked me to consider a circuit in Lincolnshire. It's just a wee circuit, and our societies are widely scattered but they want me to undertake it."

"But you'll have to leave London!" Catherine exclaimed, her face falling.

"Yes, but if I'm able to build up the circuit I may be called back here," William remarked, "or we may be able to marry within a few months and settle down there. Wouldn't you like to be a country parson's wife?"

"I'd like to be one country parson's wife — or the wife of a city parson — if the parson's name should happen to be William Booth," Catherine assured him.

CHAPTER 4

Spalding is due north of London in the county of Lincolnshire. Since it is close to the North Sea the winds blow down from Scandinavia, up the Wash, to the town and the surrounding points where William was to establish his circuit.

The situation in Spalding was just the reverse of the one in London. The people received him with open arms. Although it was a circuit and the chapel in Spalding was just one of several where William preached, he made his home in Spalding and the people could not do enough for him. He was invited to every home in his congregation — not once, but many times — for dinner.

It was a somewhat frightened young preacher who stood

before his congregation the first Sunday in November, 1852, but at the close of the service the people greeted him with such heartiness that he felt as if they were completely his own.

The following day he sent off a long letter to Catherine, saying among other things:

> I felt some nervousness when I was confronted by the large congregation. In the morning I had very little liberty; but good was done, as I afterward learned. In the afternoon we had a Prayer or After-meeting, at which one young woman wept bitterly. I urged her to come to the communion rails at night. She did so, and the Lord saved her. She afterward sent me a letter thanking me for urging her to come. In the evening I had great liberty in preaching, and fourteen men and women came to the communion rail; many, if not all, finding the Saviour.

By the next evening William was in full stride. He preached from the heart without worry and eighteen men and women came forward to the penitent-form.

There was one elderly man among them and he whispered to William, "Ah'm here to see if Christ could wash a heart as black as hell."

William suggested that they kneel in prayer, and his deep voice sounded forth in an earnest petition to God to cleanse the heart of the sinner. Others joined in the prayer until the building was fairly rocking with their petitions.

Finally, with a shout, the old man announced, "Ah'm got it. There's religion in my heart now. Praise God! Hallelujah!"

Perspiration poured down William's face. He had literally been wrestling with God for the soul of the sinner and by the time the service was over he was worn out with the exertion of preaching, since he was exceedingly active in the pulpit. His long arms gestured, flailed; his index finger pointed. That night he had a chill and was confined to bed in the home of friends for the entire week.

John Dumfries visited him and brought cheering words.

"I have talked with many of our people and they are eager to have you settle down amongst us. We would like to have you marry Miss Mumford. From what you have told us about her we are confident that you and she would make a great couple to minister in our chapel. Give it your prayerful consideration," he said.

"There is nothing that I would like more," William replied, "but I believe that we should wait and see if the circuit can support a couple."

William was unwell as he started out the following Sunday

for Donnington, but he had tried his unfailing remedy of salt water rubbed on his chest and he felt that it would see him through the day. In the afternoon he preached at Swineshead Bridge. William was kneeling with a penitent when someone touched him on the shoulder and said, "Here is a lady who has come to seek the Saviour, and now she has come to hear you, and she wants salvation, too." After talking with William she felt assured that the Lord had saved her, and went on her way rejoicing.

Before he left for the evening's engagement at Donnington some of the farmers who lived in the vicinity urged him to return on Monday evening and conduct other services during the week. William felt that the prospects of a successful series of meetings were slim, but he promised to return.

At the close of the evening meeting in Donnington he was torn between two courses of action, whether to preach at Donnington for a week or spend every evening at the Bridge. Since he had promised the farmers at the Bridge that he would hold services there he felt in honor bound to do so.

The Monday meeting was held in the large living room of a farmhouse and the following evening, too, they began their meeting there, but so many people were waiting outside that William decided to move out-of-doors. They adjourned to the bridge where he preached in the open air.

Writing about the experience to Catherine, William noted: "I shall always remember with pleasure the week I spent at Swineshead Bridge, because I prayed more and practiced more of the spirit of expectation and faith, and then saw more success than in any previous week of my life. I dwell upon it as, perhaps, the week which most effectually settled my conviction forever, that it was God's purpose to have me use the simplest means to bring souls into liberty, and to break into the cold and formal state of things to which so many of His people only too readily settle down."

As a result of his meetings in the Spalding area William came to the conclusion that he would always use the method of revivalism. He did not deprecate the preaching ministry of the settled pastor but he felt that his particular genius lay in the field of the revival and evangelistic work. Not yet in his mind, however, was the outline for a program of the Salvation Army which would develop later.

Nevertheless, one indication that there might be such a program in the offing was the frequent use of the word "Salvation" and the fact that he always wrote the word with a capital "S." Other words, such as "conversion," "redemption," or "communion," are not thus italicized. Evidently "Salvation" even then was the key word of William's thinking.

Catherine was solicitous concerning William's methods, for she wrote him on one occasion,

> Watch against *mere animal excitement* in your revival services. I don't use the term in the sense in which anti-revivalists would use it, but only in the sense which Finney himself would; remember Caughey's silent, soft, heavenly carriage; *he* did not shout, there was no necessity; he had a more potent weapon at command than noise. I never did like noise and confusion, only *so far* as I believed it to be the *natural* expression of deep anxiety, wrought by the Holy Ghost; such as cries of the jailer, etc., etc.; of such noise, produced by such agency, the more the better. But, my Love, I do think noise made by the *preacher* and the Christians in the church is productive of *evil only*. . . . I don't believe the Gospel needs such roaring and foaming to make it effective, and to some minds it would make it appear ridiculous, and bar them against its reception forever. There was nothing of this kind in that most powerful sermon ever preached by Peter on the day of Pentecost; the noise was made by the *people* pricked to the heart, and was the *effect* of that plain, powerful, but calm and reasonable appeal to their consciences, and not of Peter's own creating.

In the letters which they exchanged during William's service in Spalding, one senses William's feeling of inadequacy and the kindly way in which Catherine both criticized him and at the same time bolstered up his courage for his service.

Catherine was several months his senior. William was alternately optimistic and enthusiastic and then beset by doubts of his own abilities. Apparently he never doubted the goodness or the wisdom of God or the ability of Christ to save to the uttermost. Theological doubts never entered his mind. The only questions which arose in his thinking had to do with his own fitness or ability to measure up to Christ's call to him to serve.

But there were many times when he needed the bolstering-up of Catherine's helpful advice and counsel. Since he did not have Catherine at hand for conference he had to put his thoughts down on paper, more often at random than in any orderly sequence.

In 1854 a new voice was heard on William's circuit. William himself had invited the Rev. Mr. Richard Poole to visit his chapels. William wrote to Catherine about the impression which Mr. Poole had made upon his mind and heart and the lessons which he learned from the guest evangelist. He summed up his estimate of the man's preaching under three heads:

"First. Directness of aim. Every word and movement indicated that he was determined to bring that audience, young and old, into harmony with God, and this was to be done that very night before he parted with them if it was possible.

"Second. Simplicity of method, the simplest words, the plainest illustrations, the most homely and striking facts being used throughout the discourse.

"Third. The most direct dependence upon God for the result."

As a result of his listening to the man's preaching, which William felt was in startling contrast to his own, William determined that he needed more schooling. He felt more strongly than ever his own deficiencies, his lack of scholarship.

And it was easy to rationalize also that he should return to London to take up his studies. He was so busy that he never found time — and perhaps the available funds — to run down to London to see Catherine. And the yearning which he felt for her was only equalled by her eagerness to see him. If he went to London for further schooling he could see her often.

For this reason he informed the circuit that he was leaving for London and suggested that they seek someone to succeed him. With reluctance they agreed to accept his resignation and he made immediate plans to leave.

When William reached London he went at once to the Mumford home.

The reunion of the young lovers was everything that William could have desired. Catherine's earlier objections to physical embrace were cast aside, nor were they ever mentioned again. The idealistic young woman had become more practical during the months of their separation and sensed the heart hunger of her young minister which could be satisfied only by physical contact.

"My darling!" William murmured as he took Catherine into his arms.

Again the matter of their marriage came up but William now faced a period of study as a theological student and they decided that it would not be advisable for them to be married until he had finished his studies. But the old prohibition against loving embraces was now removed. William could now hold Catherine in his arms and plant tender kisses on her soft lips and cheeks. It was a considerable concession on her part, but once the matter was decided she was as ardent as he was.

Probably William would have spent more time calling at the Mumford home than would have been prudent if she had not laid down one condition. They would only enjoy an evening together when William was free from preaching responsibilities, and would limit themselves to stipulated days each week.

From the very first it was evident that scholarly pursuits were not for William. He had no bent in that direction, and time which should have been spent on his books William spent in prayer. When he should have been conjugating Greek verbs he would be out preaching. Yet, despite the constant calls which were made upon his time, William made some advance; and Dr. William Cooke, who had undertaken to guide him in his studies, finally decided to recommend him for the superintendency of a London circuit.

William protested that he was much too young for such an assignment and that he was quite incapable of directing the activities of preachers who were older than he. Furthermore, he decided that he much preferred preaching to what were essentially episcopal functions.

Dr. Cooke persisted. William could continue his studies, he could preach, and he could direct the work of a circuit. Dr. Cooke was confident, from his knowledge of the young man's abilities, that William was capable of doing all three simultaneously. But a compromise was finally reached. William agreed to serve as the assistant on the circuit, but an older man should be the superintendent.

William discovered, however, that the assistantship which, he had hoped, would leave him free to preach did not offer such a tempting opportunity. The superintendent who was appointed was a Rev. Mr. P. T. Gilton. William described him years later in these words: ". . . stiff, hard, and cold; making up, in part, for the want of heart and thought in his public performances by what sounded like a sanctimonious wail."

If it had not been for the fact that William could escape from the domination of his senior by outside preaching he probably would have terminated the arrangement soon after it began. But Mr. Gilton was wise enough to let William have his head in this regard and probably was also willing to have him go off on preaching missions wherever they were offered, since it brought some fame to the circuit to which he belonged.

One of the first invitations came from Lincolnshire, and

William went off like a knight to do battle with the devil in that county. When he arrived there he wrote to Catherine, "My reception has been exceedingly pleasing. Even the children laugh and dance and sing at my coming, and eyes sparkle and tongues falter in uttering my welcome. Yesterday I had heavy work. Chapel crowded. Enthusiasm ran very high. Feeling overpowering, and yet not the crash we had expected. My prospects for usefulness seem unbounded. But God knows best, and where He wants me, there He can send me. The people love me to distraction, and are ready to tear me to pieces to have me in their homes."

The success of these meetings was such that he began to receive other calls. Some of the ministers of the New Connexion objected to his journeys and the revivalist spirit which William engendered. They were conservative and orthodox in the extreme and William did not conform to the pattern which they regarded as the proper one for a minister. But they could not well object and so William was away from London more often than he was present in the city.

The financial arrangements actually worked out well for his circuit since he received more for his services than the stipend which he had been guaranteed as a salary and, since he gave the treasurer of the circuit all funds which accrued to him over and above expenses, he managed to keep these activities on the credit side of the treasurer's accounts, which made that worthy warmly inclined to his labors.

While he was away from London he sent regular reports to Catherine on the success of his meetings. He was discovering himself and finding his particular niche in the pattern of Kingdom work.

One of the most significant series of revival meetings which he held was in Staffordshire in the pottery region of England. The church which headed the list was the chapel in Henley and was the largest dissenting place of worship in all England. William did not want to undertake it, pleading his youth. But he was finally prevailed upon to embark on the mission and did so. It brought him considerable fame among the members of the Connexion.

During the course of his itineration a wedding date was decided upon. William no longer feared that he might not succeed in the pastorate and had agreed to accept a circuit. That meant that they could be settled wherever the Connexion decided, but there would be no problem of a financial nature. The sixteenth of June was chosen for the wedding date.

In his final letter to Catherine before this event should transpire he wrote:

My Own Darling Kate,

Bless you, how soon once more shall we meet again. Meet as we have never met before, with different feelings and different prospects. That which had been regarded as looming in the far-off distance now is very, very near. You are to be mine. We are to be one. Yes, *one.*

My whole soul must lie open before your gaze, and it will be. Yes! It shall be. And thou art to be my guardian watcher. And we are to commence our life *together* in one united and, I trust, continued sacrifice, for God's glory and the welfare of our fellow men. And yet in it I trust we shall be happy. Mutual forbearance, affection, heart-love, will do all things, be a talisman which will turn all our domestic anxieties and trials into bonds of love and cause of mutual joy.

You know me; I am fitful, *very*; I mourn over it, I hate myself on account of it. But there it is; a dark column in the inner life of my spirit. You know it. Bless you; I will try; but suppose I fail to make myself better, thou wilt bear with me and I will try to be all that thou desirest. I pray for help from on High. Oh, yes, God will give it me. Nay, give it us.

He closed his missive, as lovers have concluded their missives in every age and clime, with the words, "I kiss this letter many times."

When one recalls the drums and horns, the clarinets, fifes and flutes of a customary street or chapel service of the Salvation Army, it is difficult to imagine the quiet wedding which united William and Catherine. As planned, they were married on June 16, 1855, in the Stockwell New Chapel in the south of London. The minister was a Rev. Dr. Thomas, superintendent of the chapel circuit.

The congregation that day consisted of only two people in addition to the participants: Catherine's father and one of William's sisters. There was no music and the service was exceedingly simple.

When Dr. Thomas announced pontifically, "And I now pronounce you, the Rev. William Booth, and you, Catherine Mumford, man and wife until death do you part," the tall young minister, brave in a new black frock coat, and his little helpmeet were joined in a lingering nuptial kiss. All the pent-up longings in the young man's heart went into the embrace. Melted was Catherine's austerity, an austerity which came not from her warm heart but from the taboos with which she had surrounded her life.

But she had decided that it was not "sin" for man and

wife to engage in such an embrace and into it went heart and soul, dissolving the taboos until they no longer existed.

For the first and only time since he had begun to work in his boyhood, William had arranged for a week's respite from work. He had rented a cottage at Tyde on the Isle of Wight. He had even booked passage in advance on the ferry which took passengers from Portsmouth and Southampton over to the island.

As the two stood hand in hand on the deck and felt the warm breezes come in from the sea, it seemed as if they were sailing off together to Paradise.

"It's the one perfect moment of our lives, Dearest," William murmured.

"Without a single jarring note," she agreed. "Heaven must be much like this."

"Something like it, no doubt," William added, "and yet this is but a pale reflection of the heavenly kingdom."

Their honeymoon cottage was near the beach and William and Catherine established themselves comfortably in it soon after their arrival. William insisted on carrying Catherine over the threshold into the living room of the cottage.

"It's perfectly silly," Catherine objected.

William corrected her.

"Perfect but not silly," he said.

"And all of the neighbors are watching," Catherine added.

William made no move to put her down but looked up and down the lane.

"I don't see any," he replied blandly.

"Foolish! They're peeking from behind their curtains," Catherine reminded him.

"I wondered what women did in their spare time," William remarked. "I'm glad that now I know."

"Some women do that," Catherine said, "but this woman won't have any time to spare. I shall be too busy working with my husband."

"Bless you, Kate," William exclaimed. "That's wonderful. With you at my side I can conquer lions, slay demons and decisively defeat the powers of darkness."

"If you don't put me down soon, you huge monster, the shades of darkness will descend upon us before we put the house to rights," Catherine remarked primly.

"Ah, yes, my sweet," he agreed, stepping over the threshold.

A fire was already laid for them and, although it was high noon, William lit a taper and started the fire.

45

" 'Twill be cold later on," he remarked.

"No, dearest," Catherine objected. "Our love for one another is so warm that this house could never be chill."

Soon afterwards they walked together up to the market place to lay in a supply of groceries and then set out along the seashore, occasionally stopping to fling a pebble at the crisp waves, often exclaiming over a shell or a sea urchin.

"Do you know that this is the first time in my life that I have seen the sea close at hand?" William remarked. "Oh, to be sure, I've been in many seaside cities but always I have been too busy to see the sea close at hand, and now we are gazing over the vast Atlantic, on the other side of which is the United States and the tropics and the many wonderful places about which one reads in books. We must see them all sometime."

"Indeed, yes," Catherine agreed, "but there is work to be done as soon as our vacation here is finished, and I am eager to begin it with you. But some day we shall see those interesting and strange places."

As the sun began dropping toward the sea a chill wind sprang up and they turned about and walked back to their cottage.

"And now, Mr. Newly Married, comes such a trial as you have never faced before," Catherine remarked. "You have gone up against committees, you have faced hoodlums in the streets, but you have never had to sample Catherine Mumford's cooking. But now . . ."

"Now, alas," William remarked sadly, "I shall never have the opportunity to sample it."

"Oh, yes, you will," she retorted. "Tonight I shall cook for you the first meal with my own hands."

"I repeat," William returned, "that I shall never have the opportunity to sample Catherine Mumford's cooking. The cook this evening in my home will be Mrs. Catherine Booth, the charming wife of an impecunious Wesleyan clergyman."

CHAPTER 5

The week over, the young Booths plunged immediately into a revival campaign in Guernsey. Shortly before his marriage the Annual Conference of the New Connexion had freed

William from responsibility for his circuit in London and commissioned him to be a roving evangelist. It was intended that he should be used chiefly among the circuits in London but the Guernsey people had asked for his services much earlier and had a prior commitment on his time.

During the engagement Catherine became ill and when the obligation had been fulfilled he took her back to London and left her with her parents. He was pledged to other circuits outside of the city and had to meet those engagements. Catherine could scarcely bear the thought of being apart from him and William felt just as bereft of her presence.

But Catherine recovered in a few months' time and joined William at Sheffield. At about this time William's father-in-law suffered financial reverses and out of their scanty earnings William and Catherine sent him some money regularly.

But they were difficult days for the Booths as well. Catherine was in poor health and had to spend considerable time in bed. William was bothered with severe chest colds which occasionally bordered on pneumonia. Yet he would arise at night to attend his wife, fix her a hot drink of milk, or build up the fire. Catherine wrote regularly to her folks about his continual care for her welfare. Her letters were composed in part with advice to her impecunious father and reports of William's goodness to her. Catherine's father was a poor manager and, although possessed of innate business sense, was constantly in debt.

On one occasion, evidently in answer to a letter from her father, Catherine wrote: "I quite agree with you in thinking yourself well adapted for an Auctioneer, and I have faith to believe you will get into business and do *well*; keep your spirits up and don't conclude that because you cannot get away *just now* you must necessarily stay where you are all the winter. . . . I hope the enclosed order will be sufficient; we intended sending another pound but William has not written to the Committee for money, and he runs rather short just now; but if you want more, send word, as he can write in a couple of days and will with pleasure send you some."

In another letter to her mother, after asking the latter to look in a bureau drawer to see if any of William's heavy woolen underwear was worth sending, she added, "William encloses ten shillings worth of letter stamps which I presume father can easily get cash for . . . amongst his city friends; it is for you to defray the expenses in going to the Crystal Palace; now *remember!* that is what it is sent for; we both wish you to go."

47

William's mother was doing better financially in her little shop but the young couple also sent her funds occasionally. It meant scrimping and saving and watching the pennies carefully, but at William's meeting in Sheffield they had what William called a "crash." Apparently to him the word meant something like what a break-through of the sonic barrier would mean to an airman in the twentieth century. When William had a "crash" the auditorium would be filled to capacity.

So it was in Sheffield. Night after night William preached to capacity crowds. Like most English churches the chapel had a high pulpit and people would be seated on the steps leading up to it when the pews had been filled. The chapel would fill up before William arrived and he would have to step over men and women in order to reach the pulpit. Hundreds of people stood nightly on the steps of the balcony, in the aisles and in the vestibules.

In a comparatively short time William had become one of the leading evangelists of England, a country noted for its many evangelistic preachers. While offerings consisted largely of pence or half-shilling pieces or threepenny bits there were always enough people to insure large collections and the Booths no longer needed to scrimp.

When William had finished his work in Sheffield it was planned that they would take a short rest period and they decided to go to Chatsworth for this purpose. William's mother joined them there. Catherine was somewhat fearful of having the elderly woman with them, for she had heard some remarkable tales concerning her domineering ways, but the two got along beautifully together. Catherine wrote to her parents, describing her mother-in-law, "She is a very nice-looking old lady, and of a very sweet and amiable spirit."

Mrs. Booth had opposed her son's plan to enter the ministry but she was now proud of the reputation he had acquired, and made herself more than agreeable to both William and Catherine.

Their lodge was out in the country and William became acquainted with many of his neighbors. The Duke of Chatsworth, an elderly nobleman with long walrus mustaches, became especially fond of William, but critical of his vocation.

"Not the kind of work that a gentleman should be doing," he insisted. "Not a gentleman's vocation at all. You should be in the Church of England, of course, and, if you were, within a few years you'd probably be a bloomin' bishop."

"But I'm not interested in becoming a bishop," William objected. "I want to be an evangelist. That is the vocation to which I have been called. I want to win souls for Christ."

"H'mph!" the duke retorted. "Whatever that means it sounds like a frightful public sort of thing."

William smiled.

"Naturally it must be," he agreed. "Our meetings must bring together as many people as possible. We often fill chapels and halls to the walls, and people even gather in the vestibules and outside on the steps."

"It must be terribly conspicuous," the duke replied.

"Of course," said William.

Sir Joseph Paxton was much more appreciative of William's work and gave him considerable encouragement. But so did almost everyone whom William met. Since William was in the habit of greeting every person he met with a hearty, "Good day," he was soon known to all whom he encountered in the lanes and on the highways. He was a vigorous walker and his height, aquiline nose and fringe of whiskers under his chin and up to his ears made him conspicuous wherever he went.

William's next campaign had been set for Leeds in December, 1855. He was by now one of the best-known revivalists in England and was never at a loss for engagements. In fact, his services were so much in demand that he couldn't begin to fill the engagements which were offered to him. There was no thought that he should return to a circuit: He was evidently fitted especially well for evangelism and in this field he planned to continue.

When they reached Leeds William discovered that there had been almost no preparations whatsoever for his coming.

The hall where the meetings were to be held had not been cleaned. No one had been appointed to conduct the chorus choir which William had wanted. There was confusion about who was to lead the various services. William never presided himself, now that he had achieved the eminence which was his in the field of evangelism.

Too long had William been the suppliant, seeking employment, and ready to offer his services on almost any terms agreeable to the group which was willing to use him.

At Leeds the situation had changed.

"I'll not stay here," he fulminated. "Never in my life have I seen such carelessness in preparing for a series of meetings.

As for you gentlemen, — never have the effrontery to invite me to return."

The Rev. Mr. Crampton attempted to smooth William's ruffled feathers.

"Several of our people were ill. Those upon whom we had depended failed us. But we can have a good series of meetings, nevertheless. Please reconsider, Mr. Booth."

"We can never have good meetings unless the setting is right for them," William thundered. "There is no excuse for such negligence."

All the frustrations of the past came into focus here. Since William was human indeed he took out on poor little Mr. Crampton all of his resentment for slights he had suffered in the past. In Leeds, therefore, began the myth that was to accompany him throughout his life, that he was a stern martinet with the explosive disposition of a field marshal.

Upon the promise of the committee to set everything to rights William finally agreed to stay on and conduct the revival period which they wanted, and the services did much to enhance his reputation as a revivalist.

The probability is that William was just beginning to discover that there was a distinct advantage in acquiring a name for irascibility and that he resolved to trade upon it.

One other reason for his display of temper at the moment was Catherine's illness. She was suffering one of her recurring periods of disability and he had to undertake not only to be a revivalist, but a nurse as well. And, tired as he was, he was inclined to vent his spleen upon the first one who would cross him.

Because of her invalidism Catherine, too, was somewhat demanding. The good people of Leeds wanted to lionize William but Catherine fearful that if he should attend social events in the afternoon or following evening meetings he might meet some charming and designing females who would not be hampered by disabilities like her own. She, too, was altogether human and possessed of a share of jealousy.

Catherine's debility was due in considerable measure to the fact that she was expecting her first child in a short time. She was prone to worry about her condition and her ability to carry the babe until it should be born. Childbirth for her generation was always beset with many hazards. In the years of their protracted courtship she was the one to inspire faith in

William when he felt downhearted and uncertain about his abilities, but the role was now reversed.

She was inclined to magnify every little pain, and William would alternately tease her, pooh-pooh her fears, and offer her cheer. Childbirth at that time was frequently only accomplished with great difficulty, especially for women who lived sedentary lives. The poor seemed to bear their children without trouble, but the middle and upper class women often faced real hardships in childbearing.

And Catherine was an especially sensitive young woman. So William had to combine nursing and psychiatry in ministering to her. Inclined to be bluff and hearty, he became especially tender and solicitous of her condition. Yet he managed to carry on his series of meetings and watch over his wife simultaneously.

In January of 1856 Catherine felt certain that the baby she was carrying was dead, and William had some difficulty convincing her that the child was alive and that the symptoms which she experienced were those which every woman encounters when she brings a child into the world.

It would have been easier for Catherine if she had been among her own people and had had her mother at hand for counsel, but the Booths were constantly in strange situations and in those days the class of women whom the Booths met were exceedingly reticent to discuss childbirth with one another. It was regarded as something so altogether private — and, indeed, actually shameful — that it could not be discussed with others.

But Catherine survived and, on March 8, 1856, she presented William with his first-born child, a boy whom they named William Bramwell Booth, destined in later years to become fully as well-known as his father. William, writing to the Mumfords, described Bramwell — for so they called him to distinguish the youngster from his father — as "a plump, round-faced, dark-complexioned little fellow. A real beauty!" The son decidedly favored his mother in appearance, for William Booth had a long nose and the general appearance of an Arab sheik.

Bramwell was born in difficult circumstances, since his father had no regular source of income but had to depend upon the offerings which he received from his revival meetings. Nor did he have what could be called a home since his father and mother were nomads, now living in lodgings and occasionally in some large home with other people, as their guests, during a revival campaign. But always about him was bustle. Never was there the quiet, well-ordered home life which pediatricians consider necessary to the happiness and comfort of a new-born babe.

With an additional mouth to feed William worked harder than ever to support his wife and child. He was frequently ill. His sickness was due in considerable measure to the vigor of his preaching. He insisted on wearing heavy flannel underwear and, when he began his preaching, would be so enthusiastic in the proclamation of the Gospel that perspiration would stream down his cheeks. Afterwards, going out into the cold air, exhausted with his labors, he would come down with a chill.

He tried various remedies but always returned to his old favorite, cold salt water rubbed vigorously on his chest. Nothing seemed to alleviate the colds and bronchitis. Thus, much of the time during the winter, he would gasp for breath but continued his preaching, nevertheless.

William was in frequent conflict with the ministers of the New Connexion who were opposed to his flamboyant type of evangelism.

"Wait for the Lord to open the hearts of those people," they would counsel him. "Don't try to rush the Eternal. In God's own time He will open their hearts to the Gospel."

"But why should we wait? If we can win them now, how much better it would be for them," he would argue, "and, furthermore, if God can use me today why should we wait for some other means tomorrow?"

"Your whole approach lacks dignity," one of them expostulated.

"Dignity!" William exploded. "People are dying of hunger for spiritual food and you suggest that they can only be won through 'dignified' processes. I have stood too often on street corners trying to pluck brands from the burning to be willing to wait for the cozy, comfortable conversions which you evidently seek."

On one occasion he remarked to a fellow minister, "If I were in business none of you would object to quick profits. Well, man, I'm about the Lord's business and I'm making profits for Him. And no one can say that He deserves little profits after investing His Only-begotten Son for the redemption of mankind."

Originally Catherine was on the side of those who counseled waiting, but she had been completely won to the idea of William's kind of revivalism.

William faithfully attended official meetings of the New

Connexion, but there was scarcely a meeting convened in which charges, either direct or oblique, were not leveled against him.

"I'm not one to set the world afire today," one brother would piously assert. "I much prefer the slow, gradual process of evangelism which the Lord Himself employed."

"If one seeks his own glory he will carry on a program of mass evangelism," another would say, "but the slow process of growth in Christian grace is the way in which the Lord, from the beginning of time, has decreed that His Kingdom should grow.'"

"We poor preachers eke out a bare existence while *some* brothers grow wealthy, living like kings, with their daily evangelistic meetings. And these brothers bleed our congregations, leaving little for us to do our necessary work. Our good Lord was always poor. I prefer to follow in His footsteps," another would hint.

Whenever he attended conferences William was subject to direct charges or innuendo. The latter was particularly hard to face and sometimes William fired back at those who decried his methods. He did so from sincere conviction that what he was doing was the Lord's work but, undoubtedly, he also did it through pique. He was not a mild individual and he could stand only a certain measure of criticism before he would lash out at his critics.

The end result was that he antagonized most of the members of the conference. Some were conscientiously opposed to his methods. Others were irked by his dogmatism. Many were jealous of the successes which he had achieved. And there was the general criticism that the results of his program were almost nil. "Booth converts have no staying power," they said. "Let him get out of town and they lapse back into their old ways, and their spiritual condition is worse than it was at first."

Honest criticism, jealousy, conservatism, all helped to play their part in closing the doors of evangelism to the young revivalist in the New Connexion. At the Annual Conference of 1857, which was held at Nottingham, it was decided that William should cease his evangelistic labors and take over a circuit.

The vote to relegate him to a circuit was close. Forty-four decided that he should be assigned to a circuit and forty that he should continue his evangelistic labors. The conference consisted of both ministers and laymen. Most of the forty-four votes to assign him to circuit work were cast by ministers.

A letter to William from one of the laymen gives an indication of the opposition which he faced. The man wrote:

I believe that, as far as the preachers have power, they will close the New Connexion pulpits against you. Human nature is the same in every Conference, whether Episcopalian, Wesleyan, New Connexion, Primitive or Quaker. And the only way for such men as you and Caughey to escape the mental rack and handcuffs is to take out a license to hawk Salvation from the great Magistrate above, and absolutely refuse to have any other master.

O Brother Booth, if I could preach and floor the sinners like you can, I would not thank Queen Victoria to be my aunt or cousin! When I hear or read of your success, I could wish to be your shoeblack! There is no man of whom I have read, Caughey excepted, who has equalled you for usefulness considering the short time you have been at it. And for you to follow the decrees of the New Connexion Conference, or of any other conclave of men, to turn you away from following the guidance of the Holy Spirit, is what I cannot bear to think of. I know what you feel, and I also have shed the big agonizing tear, when placed in the same circumstances. Glory be to God, I am *free*, and I will keep so. You know what the wolf said to Towser, "Half a meal with liberty is better than a whole meal without it!"

William received his assignment, one of the worst possible in the conference. One reason for the type of assignment which was given him, to be sure, was that he knew nothing about conference politics and had pulled no strings to secure what would have been regarded as a desirable post. His superintendent, with whom no other man would have been willing to work, was a funereal-looking individual who regarded piety as being long-faced and somber. Brighouse itself was a smoky, unpleasant town, lying in a valley and never altogether free of smog.

There was little or no empathy between William and his superintendent. The latter was altogether unwilling to have William engage in his evangelistic work, for he had little sympathy for labors of that kind. William described the work to which he was assigned in these terms: "Labor in this circuit is most like ploughing on a rock of anything I have ever experienced in my life."

One happy result of the move, however, was that Catherine could enter upon the work of the church and assume responsibilities of her own. She began her work after the birth of her second child, Ballington. Their first-born, William Bramwell, was two years old when his brother put in an appearance.

Bramwell was a hearty child and Ballington, despite the environment into which he was born, was also sturdy and strong. But Catherine's spinal trouble returned and she often had to

54

retire to her bed immediately upon the completion of a meeting which she had arranged.

Ballington was baptized by the Booths' great friend and William's ideal, the American evangelist, James Caughey. Following the simple service the two had a long conference and Caughey gave to William the heartening which he greatly needed.

William had been on probation as a preacher for four years. The period having terminated, he was eligible for ordination. In the course of the examination William first had to give an account of his labors for the preceding period.

Before the ordination he was frank in talking with some of the conference members, objecting to the "laying on of hands" of certain of the ministers. At the same time he earnestly desired that those whom he respected and admired should have a part in the ceremony. William believed that in this rite the Holy Spirit would be imparted to him as a minister but he could not see how the hands of certain of the ministers could ever be regarded as instruments of the Spirit.

William did not demand perfection of his peers. He recognized his own shortcomings as well, but he did feel that sincerity was absolutely essential, and sincerity, he felt, should be accompanied by zeal for the winning of souls. Unless a man was zealous for the proclamation of the Gospel and eager to rescue souls from sin, William did not regard him as worthy of his calling.

William's ordination occurred in 1858. That same year he was assigned to the chapel and circuit at Gateshead. At the ordination conference some of his warmest friends came forward with the proposal that William should be reassigned to the field of evangelism. They presented the requests of a considerable number of churches that William should return to them to conduct these special services.

As a result of these importunities there was an implicit understanding that if William were successful in his pastoral duties he might be released for his beloved work. Upon that understanding he went to Gateshead where he began his pastoral work.

That same year their first daughter was born to the Booths. The child was named Catherine for her mother and she was later to be known as "the Maréchale," for she became the pioneer leader of the work of the Salvation Army in France.

Although William had not been assigned to evangelistic

work, he could not be kept from it and the Gateshead people fell in line with the idea of a strong evangelistic program.

Despite the fact that she had a family to look after and that the family was exceedingly young, Catherine felt that she should assume a share of the parish work. When she met drunken women on the sidewalks as she went to do her shopping she appealed to William.

"Perhaps I could talk to those poor forlorn creatures when I meet them and later call on them in their homes," she suggested.

"No," William replied emphatically. "You are not strong enough for this kind of work. And you can never be certain just what a drunkard, man or woman, will do. Some of them are harmless, but others might actually assault you if they took exception to that which you told them. Occasionally a drunken man wants to pick a fight with me, and you know it takes courage to do that."

"Just because no courage would be needed to assault me might make it possible for me to win over such a person," Catherine remarked sagely. "I'm sure no one, whether man or woman, would attack me."

"You don't know drunkards as well as I do," William retorted bluntly. "If you did you'd know that you can never predict what one of them will do."

But what Catherine lacked in size she made up in pure grit. She not only encountered and talked with drunkards on the streets but also went into their homes. Their condition was almost indescribable. One of the homes in which she visited was later described in her own words when she wrote: "I remember in one case finding a poor woman lying on a heap of rags. She had just given birth to twins, and there was no one of any sort to wait upon her. . . . By her side was a crust of bread, and a small lump of lard. . . . The babies I washed in a broken pie-dish, the nearest approach to a tub that I could find. And the gratitude of those large eyes, that gazed upon me from that wan and shrunken face, can never fade from my memory."

In 1860 the Booths' fifth child was born, their second daughter, whom they named Emma. Even though they were again practically penniless, the child was warmly welcomed into the home.

At about this time William fell seriously ill and had to be hospitalized for some time. Catherine, who had long championed both women's suffrage and a "female" ministry, took over William's preaching responsibilities in the church and was exceedingly well received.

One of the older members of the congregation remarked, "I thought that no one could preach like our young minister but I'm almost persuaded that his 'ooman can beat him."

His wife snapped back, " 'Tain't 'almost.' She's ever' bit as good as 'er 'usban'."

At this same time, with William in the hospital, Catherine had her hands full, for the children came down with whooping cough. Catherine kept the news from William since she didn't want him to worry about their children.

One afternoon, when she was visiting him at the hospital, he said to her, "Dearest, we probably don't have a farthing. I've been thinking it over and have about decided. . . ."

She interrupted, "Now don't worry, William. I have plenty of money for all of our needs. You can dismiss any thought of trouble. I'm getting along beautifully. And I'd also like to remind you, Mr. Preacher, that our people have said some complimentary things about my preaching."

William gave a wry smile.

"I have no doubt but what you've given them most acceptable sermons, my dear, and I'm not worrying. But I've been thinking about our future. It's almost conference time and I hope above everything else that they will let me go back to evangelism. It's the field of service where I can do the most good. It's what I should be doing all the time."

Catherine's spirits soared. William was evidently improving considerably if he was so eager to return to the work.

William continued, "But, knowing the men of the conference as well as I do, I'm afraid that they may want me to take a circuit and will not let me conduct evangelistic meetings. And if I don't, my dear, I've about made up my mind to break off with the Connexion and go out on my own."

He looked at her with such hopeful eyes that she knew she must respond favorably.

"If God wills it, William dear, and you are persuaded that this is God's call, then this is what we must do."

"Even though it leaves us penniless. . . ."

"Even though we are penniless," she said firmly. "The Lord will provide."

William took Catherine with him to the Annual Conference which was held in Liverpool in 1861. England was in an uproar at the time as a result of the Civil War which had broken out in the United States. The North had declared all southern ports to be in a state of blockade.

This meant that no cotton could be exported from the South and many English mills were shut down for lack of raw material. Since the British abhorred slavery, and decades earlier had freed the Negroes in their American colonies, the sympathies of the English people were with the North, while their strongest economic ties were with the South.

The loss of this big market presaged difficult times for the English factory towns and the ministers were aware of the probable effects upon their congregations as well. It was a difficult time to start on a crusade of evangelism, but William had made up his mind that he would do just that — with or without the blessing of the conference.

William was basically much more compromising by nature than Catherine. He would have been willing to plead his case before the conference and ready to put it in the strongest possible terms but, when it came down to the final assignments, he would undoubtedly have been ready to go where the conference would send him. Not so Catherine. While she would be slower to make a decision, once it was made she would stand by it.

To be sure, William had to think of the security of his family. Having in mind the needs of his wife and children, he was loath to take a stand which might jeopardize their welfare. But Catherine was possessed of a sturdy conviction that if one did that which was right the Lord would provide.

When William wavered, therefore, Catherine said forthrightly, "William, you know perfectly well that if you will go straight on in the path of duty, the Lord will take care of us."

"Dearest, I believe that with all my heart, but I also believe that I must be sure I am following the path of duty before I burn all my bridges behind me," William assured her.

"But you have demonstrated already where that path is," she exclaimed. "You were born to be an evangelist — not to be the minister of a chapel. In the one field you have been eminently successful — not necessarily so far as worldly goods are concerned but for the advancement of the Kingdom. But in the other field you always feel as if you are out of your element. You go through the motions of being a pastor but your bent is toward evangelism. Therefore, if the Connexion has nothing for you — or if the officers of the Connexion say there is nothing — step out of it. We will make out. Never fear."

Catherine attended the session when announcement was made of the appointments for the year. William was assigned to a single church with no provision for him to be released at any time to conduct evangelistic services.

Up in the balcony a little woman stood up when his appointment was announced and, in a ringing voice which could be heard in every corner of the chapel, said, "Never!" Catherine had spoken.

Thereupon she walked down the stairs to the floor of the chapel where she met William, and together they made their way from the conference hall.

Some of William's friends intercepted him in the vestibule.

"Don't do anything in haste," one of them urged. "Above all, man, make the decision for yourself. Don't allow Catherine to dictate what you are to do."

"The decision was mine," William explained. "But I might have compromised at the last moment. God has spoken to both of us, but only Catherine had the courage to make known to the brethren what the Lord had said to us."

"But think of the hardships you may face," the friend urged. "There is no minister who is so far lost as one without conference recognition and a conference relationship."

Catherine, who had been listening to the conversation, interrupted. "We have a relationship which is far more important than the one you esteem," she said resolutely.

"What is that?"

"A relationship to the Lord," she returned simply.

William's last act as a member of the conference was to write his letter of resignation which he closed with these words:

"Looking at the past, God is my witness how earnestly and disinterestedly I have endeavored to serve the Connexion, and knowing that the future will most convincingly and emphatically either vindicate or condemn my present action, I am content to await its verdict."

CHAPTER 6

William was now free to extend the horizon of his evangelistic efforts since he was no longer bound by Connexional ties. In this step there was a considerable measure of liberty for him but, by the same token, his independence of denominational ties was also a handicap. There was comparatively little fellowship between denominations in the 1860's. The Free Council of Churches of Great Britain was not even remotely dreamed of. While religious groups could not be described as hostile toward one another they had not as yet discovered how to work together except through foreign mission boards which were independent of denominational control but, in effect, were often sects in themselves.

The Booths decided to move to London. Catherine went on ahead and, in order to save expense, William booked passage for himself and the children by ship from Newcastle to London. When they reached Brixton and the shelter of the Mumford home they didn't have a penny left.

After spending a day seeking employment William would appear in the evening with a large parcel under his arm. "Bread — slightly old but good for the teeth," he would announce. Or he would hand over a sack of bones which he had picked up at the butcher's. "Got them for thruppence. They are useful in preparing a most nourishing beverage — soup. Good for young and old."

Because of his complete independence of denominational ties he was totally without preaching opportunities for some months. The first break in the wall occurred when the Rev. Mr. Alfred Durning, a friend in the New Connexion ministry who had a small church in Hayle, Cornwall, invited William to come with his family to open a campaign there. The prospect was meager but William's implicit faith in the maxim that the Lord would provide impelled him to go to Cornwall instead of waiting for what might have seemed a better opportunity to establish himself as an independent evangelist.

And this engagement was one which threw wide open the doors to a great revival in Cornwall. There was some difficulty at the outset with the proposal that there should be what William termed a "penitent-form." This has long been a standard device in evangelism but, basically, its use has become well-nigh universal because of William's insistence upon it.

The superintendents of the circuits were opposed to it because it tended to make the act of repentance conspicuous and they felt that repentance could be just as effective if it were not so public. But William argued that if sinners were willing to repent they should be eager to tell the world about their repentance. In many respects, during the years of his evangelistic services, William was forging the techniques which he later employed in the Salvation Army. And one of those techniques was the penitent-form or mercy seat.

The superintendents of the Cornish churches where William held his revival campaigns finally agreed to this innovation, albeit reluctantly.

But if William exhibited to the world supreme self-confidence in his preaching and services he was far from feeling it. He was still uncertain that he had done the right thing in literally defying his brethren by cutting himself off from the Wesleyan Connexion. After all, who was William Booth to set himself against the judgment of his peers?

In the journals in which he wrote conscientiously every day there is mention made of the pains that racked his body and then a notation: "Opened my eyes this morning with strong desire for more of the Holy Ghost in my own heart. Felt some little power in private. I want more."

Occasionally, too, he would slip off to revival services which were held in the church at Pendeen with a well-known evangelist, the Rev. Robert Aitken, conducting the services. When he did William would drink in the words of the preacher and then remain long afterwards in the pew, his eyes filled with tears, as he prayed in the agony of his own soul.

The revival in Cornwall was outstanding, perhaps especially so because of William's own need for the presence of the Holy Spirit. As he preached he did so out of a personal agony of soul. Here was no perfect saint preaching to sinners but one who felt himself "chief among sinners," preaching to others in like condition, sensing their frustrations and their needs.

As a consequence the Cornwall revival became phenomenal. Villagers tramped daily for miles to attend the services. Fishermen came for eight or ten miles, rowing their skiffs across the open sea, to be present. In some places business came to a standstill. In the town of St. Just it was recorded that more than a thousand persons were received into membership in the different churches.

But there were repercussions. The Wesleyans passed resolutions in their conferences closing their doors to the Booths. The Primitive Methodists took official action urging their churches "to avoid the employment of revivalists, so called." If he had had hopes that he might renew his relationship ecclesiastically with the Methodists his hopes were dashed by these actions.

It should be noted, however, that much of the objection

to William's revival methods was due to the intense emotionalism which accompanied them. People fell to the floor fainting. They shouted for joy. As they engaged in prayer it was often bedlam as many prayed at one time, or spoke in tongues. Many earnest Christians felt that this emotionalism had in it no content of true religion. Genuine religion should be basically intellectual — not emotional. Hence William Booth came in for considerable criticism — not only at this time but throughout his life.

On the other hand, William was inclined to doubt the validity of a religious conversion which did not have a strong emotional content. In later years he was to receive the eager support of people from almost all of the evangelical churches, but at the time he was greatly criticized, particularly from the ranks of the New Connexion group of Wesleyans of which he had been a part.

As usual, the Booths found themselves in difficult straits financially, but there would occasionally be large gifts in the collection plates, or some friends would come forward to relieve their financial problems. It almost seemed as if they were always on the verge of disaster and then were helped out of it by the guiding hand of God.

The Connexional ministers and Primitive Methodist clergymen carefully arranged matters so that, although their laymen were eager to open their chapel doors to the Booths, the doors were kept closed against them. However, one last opportunity came to them and this was at Redruth where the Free Methodists invited them to come. William preached there for some weeks until, in February, 1863, he was invited to go to Cardiff.

Some chapels were open to them but the majority were closed. For this reason they began a new procedure which was later to be followed in their work in the Salvation Army. Instead of renting churches and chapels they would rent premises which were used for secular purposes. This meant that one more chasm was dug between the Booths and the organized church for, although they closed their doors to the Booths, many of the churches objected to their using such premises.

Their first venture in this field was when they acquired a medium-sized circus tent, set it up, arranged for seats, and started their meetings. It is possible that this was the first time in the history of revivalism and evangelism that a tent meeting was held. But it proved an exceedingly successful mission. Tents could be used only for a few months during the summer, yet this first summer William's emotionalism found an answering chord in the hearts of the volatile Welshmen who came out in great crowds.

Among those who were won to Christ at the tent meetings were John and Richard Cory. John was a wealthy coal mine operator.

"Aa never found the good Lord until ye come," he remarked to William. "Aa'm like that pooblican, Zacharias, who was oop the tree. An' like him Aa want to give back to the Lord a part o' what I owe Him. Ye must take from me what ye need for y'r work. Aa'll not take 'No' for an answer."

William was not at all disposed to return a negative reply to any offer of financial aid, for he was always pressed for funds to pay rent and food bills. In considerable measure the Corys and a Mr. and Mrs. Billups provided for William and Catherine the funds with which to carry on their ministry.

Finally, as it became colder, the tent meetings attracted fewer people and William and Catherine decided to accept an invitation to go to Walsall for a series of meetings. When they arrived there they discovered that the enthusiasts who had urged them to come had made no arrangements for them.

Mr. and Mrs. Will Folsum assumed that the chapels would be open to them but they had made no efforts to secure preaching points. Again the Booths were down to their last shilling but this time William became seriously ill and this added to the complexities of their situation.

Once more they decided that the family would have to split up. Catherine would return to London. William would go to Sheffield and make it his headquarters. This he did, but was exceedingly lonesome for the presence of his family. In one letter he asked Catherine to send him "a little love talk" which he could carry in his purse. He always burned most of Catherine's letters after reading them but would always keep one particularly affectionate epistle with him as a reminder of their love for each other.

One of his own typical family letters which the Booths preserved was this: "Tell Willie I got him a penknife this morning and inform Ballington that I am going to try to get him little white mice. The white mice and pigeon man is coming with the Hallelujah Band to Leeds. I have not time nor patience to write more. Somehow I am nervous, the day is damp and sultry, and my room is hot and close, and I am out of sorts for writing. I don't like the folks much I am with and I am tired. I shall do better in the morning."

Destitute as he was, he still found the wherewithal to get to Leeds to see the white mice and pigeon man. But William was not only interested in white mice for Ballington. He wanted to see what this specialist in rodents did in a religious service, for the Hallelujah Band was a troupe of wandering evangelists who would do almost anything to attract a crowd.

In later years, speaking to a group of workers, William remarked, "Never be afraid to do the extraordinary to win a hearing. But be honest. Don't advertise that you're bringing an elephant to town when all you have is a donkey. Remember that you are dealing with the unchurched and the unsaved. They may not be curious to know the way of salvation but they will be curious to see something unfamiliar, and yet familiar enough so that they have heard about it. And, above all, don't be afraid to make a noise to attract people."

Again he noted, "Jesus was probably criticized for gathering crowds about him, for preaching on street corners and hillsides, for healing the sick and feeding the hungry — just as we are criticized. And never forget that his enemies said of Him, 'He is a friend of publicans and sinners.' So must we be known."

William was kept sufficiently occupied with preaching in Sheffield to bring in a small amount of money and some of his friends also set aside funds on a monthly or quarterly basis to aid him. Some of the funds so received were outright gifts but some were in the form of loans.

Late in 1864 the sixth child was born, a girl who was named Marian. Mrs. Booth had scarcely enough funds to raise five children and a sixth made an additional mouth for which it was difficult to make adequate provision, but the child was welcomed as had been all the others.

Although preoccupied with her children and the financial problems of providing them food, Catherine listened to a committee from Rotherhithe in Southeast London, one of the most noxious slums of the metropolis. The committee members invited her to come and conduct evangelistic services of the same type that William carried on.

She had moved to Leeds in 1865 to be with William. They decided that they had been apart too long, and that it would be a saving if the family could be together. William was conducting revival services in and around Leeds and she was managing the home. It was good to be with William again and he thoroughly enjoyed playing with the little ones during the weeks when he was at home. Often he was free only in the mornings but he poured out his affection upon the children.

Catherine wrote to her parents about the indifference of the churches and the growing conviction that they would ultimately decide that their real mission lay in the teeming slums of the city. The invitation to Rotherhithe, although tendered to Catherine and not to William, seemed like a call from God.

Actually it came about as something of a "stunt." The minister decided that he needed something startling and bizarre to attract crowds. What would be more novel than to have a woman conduct the mission, and who could equal Catherine Booth? Women preachers were unheard of, although in later years two of the Booth daughters were to become world famous preachers: Catherine, who was to found the Salvation Army in France; and Evangeline, familiarly known as "Eva," who was in later years to become the general of the Army and one of the most outstanding and dynamic woman preachers of all time.

William was somewhat piqued by the invitation.

"I wonder why they didn't invite me?" he inquired of Catherine. "I would have been available."

"I'll write and tell them that you can come. They probably didn't know that you were free," she replied. "Why should I go when your preaching would be so very much more effective?"

"You'll do no such thing," he objected with ready practicality. "They might not want me, and just possibly they may suggest that they don't want you if you embarrass them by demanding that they take me. No. You had best make up your mind to go, Catherine."

"But what about the children?" Catherine inquired.

"I've taken care of them before," he reminded her.

"But not the baby."

"No, not this particular infant," he agreed, "but if I remember rightly every one of the other children started out exactly like this one; eating regularly and making raucous outcries if the meal was not ready on time, wetting diapers, waking up in the middle of the night to bawl. Oh, yes, darling, have you not also noted that they definitely possess their father's strong voice, and not their mother's gentle one?"

"Tush!" Catherine replied with a smile. "And I assume that you will also insist that they have dispositions just like their father's: sunny, kindly, sweet, etc."

"I was just about to add that," William admitted, "except for the phrase that you tacked on at the end. Just what does that 'and so forth' stand for?"

"Oh, you know," Catherine replied airily, "— stubborn, opinionated, mulish, and the nicest husband a woman ever had."

"Again, except for the last phrase, I'm inclined to agree with you," William admitted, giving her a warm hug and a resounding smack on her cheek. "Then you'll go, darling?"

"I suppose I must."

Catherine's mission was exceedingly successful. Her popularity as a preacher was due, no doubt, to the innovation of a woman in the pulpit. Just as P. T. Barnum advertised the Cardiff Giant as something altogether unique and astounding, so the sponsors of her mission noted the astonishing fact that a person of the gentler sex, whose precincts were supposedly the kitchen or nursery, was to be the speaker. Handbills with this caption, "COME AND HEAR A WOMAN PREACH," were distributed broadcast throughout the area.

Catherine wrote daily to William while he struggled with housekeeping problems, and he also gave her a running account of the day's activities in his letters. He had faced housekeeping duties before when he had shepherded his little flock from time to time in Newcastle, and then he had taken the children by sea to London, but never for as protracted a period. Catherine was so well received that the meetings were extended from two weeks to four, and then to six.

William also encountered some problems in budgeting. Since the family was always on the brink of poverty this was no new experience, but he had grumbled at the expenses of housekeeping as do most husbands, and wondered what Catherine did with all of the money that he gave her for this purpose. But when he found that he was being called upon to repair shoes, buy writing tablets for the children's school work, and take care of the constant little expenditures which seemed to come up every few minutes, he discovered that Catherine had done well.

Perhaps, by way of encouraging Catherine to cut the meetings short, in one of his letters he wrote: "I have been very poorly. I have had to shut out the children since breakfast. My head has been so very bad; it is a little better. I went supperless to bed at ten o'clock, in the hope of getting a refreshing night's sleep, but was disappointed. I was awake very early, feeling dreadfully."

But William had all of the children spic and span when the train, bearing Catherine, arrived in Leeds.

Catherine flew into his arms.

"My poor darling!" she murmured. "Was it too hard for you to look after the children all this time?"

William held her at arms' length.

"Not at all," he replied. "Not at all. We got along beautifully. Housekeeping is really mere child's play. But what about you? You probably discovered what a difficult grind it is to prepare a sermon a day and preach night after night, didn't you?"

"Oh, no, dearest William," she replied airily. "It was really a vacation for me. It was such a rest to get away from cooking and darning, baking and cleaning. . . ."

Ballington interrupted.

"Mumsey," he remarked, "could you darn my stockings first? I don't think there's a pair left without holes in the toes or heels."

"But didn't your father . . ." she began.

William hastily interrupted.

"I drew the line at darning," he explained. "Making meals, cleaning the house, I was most adept at those tasks. But I felt sure that you would rather take over that minor chore when you returned."

"I'll soon have things to rights," she agreed dryly. "It won't take long."

William heaved a sigh of relief. He believed that women should have equal rights with men. Women should be preachers or evangelists if they so desired and felt the call of God to enter the ministry. But he was convinced that, so far as housework was concerned, he didn't want men to have equal rights — or responsibilities — with women. It was good to have Catherine back with the family again.

They sat in their little parlor that night as Catherine told William about her experiences. She came finally to speak of the decision which she had made.

"We are needed in London," she urged. "If there is poverty in other cities it does not compare with that of the metropolis. If there is sin elsewhere it is not of the magnitude that I encountered in London. And the churches seem quite unconcerned. If they hold Sunday services that is enough. The non-conformists don't even keep their chapels open for prayer during the week. At least the Angelicans and the Roman Catholics provide a place of refuge for people in need."

"I have felt the same way, dear," William said, "but I have wondered whether I could do anything to fill the need. True, I have had some success as an evangelist, but do I have the ability to cope with the situation in London? To go there and feel that the work I would be doing would be of no avail, to feel that I couldn't measure up to the need, that is what holds me back."

"You can't cope with London's problems all by yourself, dearest," Catherine replied, "but God can. And I am convinced that He could use you there. I know that He used me and I am confident that what I did you could do ten times better."

William was gratified but he protested mildly.

"Ah, no, dear, yours was a fresh voice and a new approach. If I can equal what you did I will be well satisfied. You were truly wonderful."

"And if I was, it was because I felt the power of God surging through me, the Spirit of God speaking to my heart, and because I knew that your prayers were supporting me," Catherine affirmed.

"I prayed for you night and morning," William replied.

"I could feel it all the time."

"And now, what about London?" William asked. "You feel that we should go there?"

"Most decidedly."

"We may find it difficult to make both ends meet," William reminded her. "It costs more to live in London than here."

"Of course it does," Catherine agreed, "and we will encounter many difficulties. But our Heavenly Father cares for the grass of the field, and watches a sparrow's fall. Will He not also have His eye on us?"

"I'm sure He will, but how do we know that this is where He would send us?"

"Because of the need," Catherine insisted, "a need that the churches are not meeting, a need that is not being met by anyone else. Probably darkest Africa would be easier than London's east side but the need is certainly as great here as on the dark continent."

"Well, then, let's go," William suddenly announced. "Let's get our packing done and set out for the city. I almost feel like Dick Whittington — save that I never expect to be London's lord mayor."

"No," Catherine agreed, "that you will never be: but you will be doing that for London which no lord mayor could ever accomplish."

CHAPTER 7

The year 1865 is generally regarded as the birth date of the Salvation Army, but the Army was not known by that name until much later. And the preaching mission groups out of which the Army was built antedated 1865 by many years.

In a sense the beginnings of the Salvation Army dated back almost two centuries when Huguenot weavers fled France to escape persecution, and settled in Spitalfields and Bethnal Green near London. Others of this same group fled to North Ireland where they established the linen industry in and near Lisburn, Lurgan, and other towns in the interior of Ulster. The Huguenots set up in London an organization which they called "La Communauté." This later came to be known as "The Christian Community."

As this section of the ever-expanding metropolis of London finally became a notorious slum, it was still the center of work for the Christian Community. John Wesley had been much concerned about the welfare of the people in this area of the city and had appointed missioners to work there. Later still, the Society of Friends established a work in the neighborhood. None of them made an impact on the area sufficiently vital to change its character.

The situation in this section of the city was aptly described by the coroner for Middlesex who reported that "the sickness and destitution prevailing were scarcely to be believed except by eye-witnesses." In round terms he denounced the shameful neglect of sanitary boards, and the criminal conduct of water companies which had brought about the disgusting condition and arrangement of water supply, drainage and closets.

He added that there were houses without waterbutts or dustbins, cellars full of putrid rubbish, rooms which had not been whitewashed for thirty years. In one house where forty-one persons were living, the water supply of only eighteen gallons was kept in a cask alongside a dustbin. One other instance cited more than fifty people who were dependent upon one small pipe which was turned on for only an hour or two daily.

The first impact of William Booth upon London was in a dilapidated tent which was set up in an abandoned cemetery on a side street in Whitechapel, Sunday afternoon, July 2, 1865.

The churches of the Connexion had been closed to William but the East London Special Services Committee had heard enough about William's ability as a preacher to feel that he was the man who could best open up a preaching mission in this area of teeming poverty. The trustees of the cemetery, according to their minute book, had voted permission a year before for a tent to be erected in the burial ground for "the purpose of religious services amongst the poorer classes not in the habit of attending any place of worship."

While services were held at that location for almost a year before William preached there for the first time, the success of such meetings was indifferent. William brought to the project the fire and enthusiasm needed to make the services effective. The very first Sunday five people came forward.

William met with them afterwards for more than an hour to instruct them in the meaning of the Christian faith. Then he started out for home. Arriving, he found Catherine waiting anxiously for him.

"I was afraid that something might have happened. It is such a bad section of the city," she vouchsafed.

"I didn't even think of that," he replied. "But we broke through tonight. I got five souls for the Kingdom. I stayed for some time afterwards to give them instruction. We had a glorious victory, dear, and I have fully decided that we must remain here. I have truly found my destiny."

From that tent, through several changes of location and method, there is an unbroken line which leads eventually to the Salvation Army and its world-wide mission, for out of the tent meetings grew The Christian Mission in East London, and eventually the Salvation Army itself.

William now had to call upon the techniques which he had learned in his street meetings years before. This came about because the tent meetings were akin to them in character and quite unlike the chapel revival services which William had been holding for the previous several years.

"They shout their objections to the points I make, Catherine," William explained. "I'm carried back to my youth again. Oh, it was wonderful. We had a crash."

"Truly, it must have been stimulating to have them take exception to the preaching of the Gospel," she remarked with light sarcasm.

"Oh, but it is," William stoutly insisted. "It means that I'm not preaching to wooden logs the way I so often did in my indoor revival services. Remember, darling, that oftentimes the hearers in the chapels went to sleep while I was preaching."

"Oh, no, William. You exaggerate," Catherine protested.

"I do not. The saints actually have lulled themselves to sleep during my services. But now I'm facing sinners once again, and, believe me, I don't let any of them take protracted naps. Besides, we don't have enough benches for the crowd, and those which we do have, don't have any backs. They can't go to sleep without falling off onto the ground. Oh, it's glorious."

"What's glorious — the lack of backs?" Catherine inquired.

"No, of course not," William retorted. "It's the response."

"You mean their shouted objections?"

"No, I mean the fact that something happens. The meetings are alive, sparkling. They fairly crackle."

"But is that what your committee wants? Aren't there a number of Friends among those who are sponsoring the services? You don't mean to say that they approve of your meetings? I thought that they awaited the Spirit in quiet. And no one could ever accuse you of being a quiet preacher."

William laughed.

"No. I'm not quiet. That's quite true," he agreed. "But those Quakers — bless their hearts — are able to recognize the presence of the Holy Spirit when He blesses our preaching. He may come to them personally in quiet fashion, but they know that He must come to those poor folk as a mighty rushing wind. You see, Catherine, the Spirit comes to different people in different ways."

"You wouldn't recognize His presence if He came to you as He comes to the Quakers, would you?"

"I'm sure I would," William replied. "And He often comes to me in quiet, but I don't think that He wants me to be quiet when I'm preaching. And, of course, I wouldn't know how to be."

William was right about that — but only partly right. His preaching wouldn't have been as effective as it actually was if he had merely shouted. But he was a preacher who was born to preach. He could shout with the best of the evangelists but he could also drop his voice down in register until it sounded like a placid stream flowing through a meadow, and not a rushing torrent fighting its way down a canyon. He played on his voice as the harpist plays upon his instrument, as a capable organist brings forth melody from a series of pipes. He could play quietly and then suddenly burst forth into a crescendo of sound. And the people loved it and responded.

Financially the Booths were no better off than they had been before. When William was engaged in evangelism in the chapels the offerings which were taken usually managed to keep the family — if not in comfort, at least from starvation. But the offerings which were taken in the tent meetings were negligible. However, funds were supplied him — albeit in limited amounts — by the East London Special Services Committee. But rarely were the appropriations able to keep up with the needs.

If the attendance at the tent showed any signs of slumping William would open a meeting on a street corner and, after a crowd had gathered, would start out for the tent, the group singing hymns as the people marched along. William had to accommodate his long stride to the shuffling feet of people whose shoes were so worn out and misshapen that they could scarcely step out in them without dropping their footwear from their feet.

Often William held these open air meetings on what was then known as the Mile End Waste but is now called Bethnal Green.

Quite naturally William's favorite hymn was, "Onward, Christian Soldiers, Marching As to War," and he would lead out in the song, always in march time.

"Don't drag it," he would shout. "Sing out."

Others, too, held meetings on Bethnal Green, as in Hyde Park in the twentieth century, advocating everything from free love to the destruction of the British Empire. Pseudo-Hindus in dirty turbans pointed out the advantage of believing in Krishna, and the forerunners of communism advocated the destruction of all forms of government so that people could live in freedom. Many of William's most potent illustrations came from the extravagant statements of advocates of atheism for he combatted them vigorously.

So successful was he that many of these speakers suggested to their followers that one sure way to stop this preacher was to use rotten eggs and overripe vegetables, but nothing daunted William.

"The fool hath said in his heart that there is no God," he

72

declaimed, "and there are many fools who are preaching to you that the Almighty is not. How they can say that to you when all about you are green grass and flowers which God has made, and when you, who were made in the image of the Almighty, are living testimony to His great power, is more than I can understand."

This was not only an answer to agnostic preaching, but it was his reply as well to decaying produce when it was hurled at him.

In his tent meetings there was little disorder of the kind that he met on the street, although occasionally a crowd of hoodlums would attempt to disrupt the meetings. Most of his opposition came when he was out in the open air, for his tormentors had no easy means to escape from the confines of the tent.

One Saturday William suggested to Catherine that they should pack a picnic lunch and go to Hyde Park, taking the children along.

"I should like to have them hear you preach there," she said, "but what about the youngest children? Will not your service be over long for them?"

"Oh, but there'll be no preaching there today," he announced. "We'll just eat and play in the park."

"That would be wonderful," she said. "It seems years since we have had a picnic."

"It has been years, dearest," he agreed. "I don't think we've done it since those days that we spent on the Isle of Wight, just after we were married."

"Well, then, it's about time," she said.

William rented a span of horses and they started off in mid-morning in an open carriage.

"Just think!" Catherine murmered. "We're actually out driving just for pleasure. But don't you think it is quite wicked to fritter away our time in this fashion — to say nothing of the rental of this rig?"

"No, I don't," he replied expansively. "You'll recall, my dear, that after the Lord had spent a week creating the heavens and the earth, the seas and all of the creatures which inhabit them, the birds of the air and the beasts of the field, and man himself, that He rested on the Sabbath Day."

"But is this rest?" she inquired anxiously.

"Possibly not for you, but it is a wonderful rest for me," he asserted.

They had a wonderful day in the park. They played hide-and-seek among the trees, they skipped pebbles in the lagoon, and they consumed a most hearty repast. William sighed as he downed the last morsel of food that was set before him.

"I declare," he said. "I had no idea that I had such a voracious appetite."

After lunch William took the older children for a walk while Catherine stretched out the younger ones on the grass for naps. William and the older Booths strolled about for some time until they glimpsed the towers of Buckingham Palace.

"What is that building?" Ballington inquired.

"It's the palace of the queen," his father replied.

"You mean she lives in a house as big as all that?"

Bramwell answered him.

"Of course she does," he said. "Queens and kings always live in enormous palaces."

"But that one is enormously enormous," Ballington countered.

"You see, she doesn't live there all by herself," William explained. "There are many other people there also, in addition to herself and her family — maids, cooks, butlers, footmen, coachmen, and so on. The queen lives in only a small part of it."

"It still seems rather large," Ballington insisted.

"I'll tell you what we'll do," William suggested. "You see those sentries marching up and down around the palace. Well, they are changed every four hours, but there is a new company which comes on duty every twenty-four. This change should occur at about four or five o'clock, I believe, probably four. We'll come back here with Mama and the other children and watch while the men now on duty are relieved."

"What's 'relieved,' Father?" asked Bramwell.

"Changed, son, changed. One company goes off duty and the men march back to their barracks. Another company of soldiers comes on to take their places."

"Oh, that would be capital fun!" exclaimed Ballington.

When they had returned to the family William explained to the others what was planned.

"But the children will be tired out by that time," she objected. "And, besides, I brought nothing along for tea."

"We can always get the ingredients from a vendor," William explained.

"Well, I must confess that I should like to see it myself," Catherine admitted.

However, William possibly regretted his decision, for every

few minutes one of the children would inquire whether the time had not yet arrived for the ceremony. He assured them that they would reach the Mall in plenty of time to observe the change, but the afternoon went all too slowly for the enthusiastic children. Finally, when he judged that it was time for them to take up a vantage point so that all might see, he loaded the family in the carriage and set out for the palace.

Neither William nor Catherine had ever witnessed the change before since they had always felt they were too busy. They reached a location reasonably close to the palace and he fastened the big iron weight to the bridle of one of the horses.

"It would be a good idea to put on their feed bags," William observed. "They might be frightened by the trumpets, but if we give them something to eat they should be all right."

William helped Catherine and the girls descend from the carriage and the family walked to a point where they could observe the ceremony to the best advantage.

"Will the queen be present?" Ballington inquired.

"I doubt it," William replied, "although I suspect that the royal family sometimes watches from the balcony."

"Is the queen our monarch, Father?" the younger Catherine asked.

"Yes, indeed," William assured her.

"Well, then, while we are waiting why don't we go up to the palace and call on her?" she inquired.

"It would be great fun playing with a prince," Ballington observed.

"I'm sure that she would welcome us," Mrs. Booth observed, realizing that William was about to be overwhelmed with questions, "but if everyone in the kingdom wanted to call there just wouldn't be room in the palace. For that reason, you see, people only call there when they're invited to come."

"Seems a silly thing," Bramwell remarked. "No one would ever visit us if they had to wait to be asked."

Ballington noticed a soldier in his tall black busby, resplendent in his red uniform.

"There's one of the soldiers, Father," he remarked.

"Yes, they're stationed all around the palace," William said.

"But why do they need guards?" Bramwell inquired. "To keep people out? It doesn't seem the nice thing to do."

"Well, maybe it's also to keep the young princes and princesses in," William observed.

The guard began to form and now from near and far people

hurried to find places from which they could observe the ceremony. Suddenly there was a ruffle of drums and soldiers formed into two straight lines, shoes and belts gleaming, heads up, chins in.

William looked about him. There must have been thousands awaiting the colorful ceremony.

"All these people!" he exclaimed.

"What did you say, dearest?" Catherine asked.

"I just said, 'All these people!'" William remarked.

"What of them?"

"Why are they here?" William asked. "Certainly not just to get a glimpse of the queen. They say she rarely appears for guard mount. Perhaps it's the music, maybe the uniforms, possibly the fine way in which the soldiers march. Look at those straight lines."

The band stopped playing for the moment and officers, smart in their gold braid, red tunics and black trousers, walked up and down the lines, inspecting the guard. The inspection completed, the sergeants made their reports, and commands were snapped. The entire contingent stood at attention, and then the military band burst forth with "God Save the Queen." People everywhere within earshot of the music stood and bared their heads as Britain's national anthem was played.

As the music stopped the guard marched sharply away, broke up into detachments, and men exchanged posts with those who had been on duty, the retiring sentries falling in behind the new detachment.

"It's a thrilling sight, isn't it?" William remarked to Catherine. "And all for a little queen — but she probably didn't even see it. Why shouldn't there be an army to serve the King of kings?"

Reflectively he sang in a low voice,

"Like a mighty army moves the Church of God:
Brothers, we are treading where the saints have trod."

He paused for a moment, and then remarked to Catherine, "But the Church doesn't march like that. It limps along. Christians don't even march in step. Each one sets off in his own way, marching hither and yon. True, we have a Captain, but we all interpret His orders differently. Why not a Christian army?"

"Yes, dear," Catherine absently replied.

CHAPTER 8

The years of the London beginnings were difficult. After one year of service the membership in the Christian Revival Union, which was the name of the organization employing William, was only sixty. William encountered the same kind of situation which every new work produces. There were those who, in the white heat of a decision for Christ, seemed ready to undertake genuine service for the Master, starting out with considerable zeal, but after attending a few meetings they would fall by the wayside.

This was due in part to theological differences between William and some of his co-workers. They disapproved of William's penitent-form.

"We cannot stomach it, Mr. Booth," Irvin Galway remarked. "It's too conspicuous. Making people come forward to indicate that they have repented and accepted Jesus Christ makes a public show of the step. Why don't you just have them raise their hands when all eyes are closed? Then you will know who has made a decision, and God will know."

"Well, for that matter, I don't suppose that an unlifted hand is really necessary to inform God of that which is in the heart of a repentant sinner," William remarked dryly. "I suspect that He can see into the soul of a man and knows whether the man's repentance is real or just the impulse of the moment."

"Yes, I suppose so," Mr. Galway agreed stiffly. "And what, then, is the purpose of the penitent-form?"

"To let everyone know," William replied decisively. "Once a man publicly commits himself there is no turning back. If he accepts Christ as his Saviour, let him get up and say so."

"It's not a good Scriptural method," Galway protested. "Nicodemus was converted by Jesus in the dead of night on a housetop."

"And another five hundred or more were converted on the day of Pentecost — and everyone knew they had salvation," William replied.

A less determined individual would have been dismayed at the response to his penitent-form proposal. Not so William.

He had had a stern school of training in the past which stood him in good stead. Altogether uncompromising, he couldn't accommodate his preaching to the theological positions of co-workers or supporters. In nonessentials — as he regarded them — he was quite willing that his fellow workers and supporters should believe as they would. But he regarded as altogether fundamental the need for a definite, public decision for Christ on the part of those who wanted to be numbered among the followers of the Master.

However, although his theology was altogether different from that of the Friends who allowed him to use their abandoned cemetery as a meeting place, he worked well with them. He was probably able to do so because he felt them to be absolutely sincere and honest in their convictions: And he was always able to work with sincere and earnest people who were followers of Christ even though they arrived at their theological postions by routes different from his own.

One of the most consecrated workers to serve with him was James Flawn who was converted the first night of his services in East London. Flawn never could stand before a crowd and offer his testimony as William hoped that all of his converts would do. He was, instead, a server of tables. The second night after his conversion he came early to the tent to see that the benches were all properly arranged and from that time on this became his self-appointed task and his contribution to the cause.

He also insisted that William come to the milk bar which he owned in Pudding Lane for refreshments. He wanted to serve luncheon daily to his hero, but William would accept only a cup of cocoa since he always brought his own food to his appointments.

Two weeks after the services had begun William was supping in Flawn's establishment when he inadvertently tripped a customer who was passing his table. William's legs were so long that they extended out into the aisle and the man stumbled over them.

"Cahn't yer keep yer toothpick legs where they belong?" the man grumbled as he picked himself up from the floor.

"I'm sorry, my friend," William apologized. "The good Lord just made me too long for comfort."

"Quite all right," the fellow replied, "so long as yer didn't do it a-purpose."

"I can assure you that I didn't; but sit down and let me

order you a cup of cocoa," William offered. "It's the least I can do to make amends."

"Nothing stronger?" asked the man.

"Nothing stronger," William assured him.

"Well, I don't mind if I do," the man said. "Couldn't take nothin' stronger anyways. I'm in trainin', you know."

"Will you bring my friend a cup of cocoa?" William asked Mr. Flawn.

Mr. Flawn came over with a steaming hot mug of the dark fluid.

"Do you two know each other?" Mr. Flawn asked.

"We met unceremoniously," William remarked.

"He tripped me — but not deliberate," the man vouchsafed.

"Well, maybe I should make you known to one another," Flawn offered.

Indicating William, he said to the man, "This is the Rev. Mr. William Booth, the evangelist who has come down to Mile End to preach the Gospel."

"The saints preserve us!" the man exclaimed. "You selected a rough spot, Reverend."

"But those people need the Gospel, don't they?" William asked.

"None need it worser," the man replied.

"Already his influence is being felt," Flawn told the fellow. "But I didn't tell Mr. Booth who you were. Mr. Booth, this is Peter Monk, a chap who hails from Ireland and has already made a name for himself in the squared circle."

"The squared circle?" William inquired.

"Aye," Peter Monk acknowledged. "The squared circle is the prize ring. And, if I say so meself, I'm not so bad as a heavyweight. But maybe you don't approve of prize fighters."

William sized him up. Sloping shoulder in the best ring tradition, hands which were covered with short, bristly hair and were as big as hams, nose and ears which had evidently suffered somewhat in past forays. William smiled broadly.

"If I didn't approve, Mr. Monk," William remarked, "I'm sure I would hesitate to tell you so. But one of the greatest saints of the Early Church was evidently very much of an athlete, and perhaps something of a boxer, too. Paul was his name and he was a personal choice of the Lord to be His apostle to the Gentiles. And what was good enough for our Master, Jesus, should be good enough for me."

"I had never heard that he was a boxer," Pete Monk remarked. "Ye're not just makin' it up, belike?"

"No, indeed," William assured him. "If ever there was a Christian athlete it was the Apostle Paul. He said, 'I have fought the good fight; I have finished my course; I have kept the faith.' May that be said of you some day!"

"I doubt that it will," Peter Monk replied. "I'm not much for religion, you know. Fightin's more my line."

William's face lighted.

"I think you'll discover that fighting is very much my line, too," he remarked. "But come to our tent and see if what I have to say is worth hearing."

"Oh, aye," Peter Monk agreed, "but I'll not promise you that I'll be one of your converts."

"I wouldn't want you to be," William assured him. "Besides, I don't make converts. God does. I don't want anyone to join up with me: Instead, I hope that people will join up with God."

"I'll be there some evenin'," Peter promised, ". . . pervidin' I don't have a fight booked to keep me away."

William thought no more about the incident. He was accustomed to hearing people promise to come to meetings and then have them fail to put in an appearance.

But the following Sunday night he almost wished that he had a man like Peter Monk at hand. A crowd of some forty hoodlums invaded the tent. They arrived soon after the first hymn had been announced. William started to read a Scripture lesson.

"What rot!" someone shouted from the rear of the tent.

William raised his head.

"Listen to these words," he said quietly. "They are for you. You need them."

"Tommyrot!" the fellow retorted.

"Tommyrot!" several others shouted.

William held up his hand for silence.

"Tommy, tommy, tommyrot!" voices in the rear of the tent began to chant.

Others took it up. "Tommy . . . tommy . . . tommyrot!"

William attempted to continue the reading. It was all to no avail.

He had faced young toughs before on the street corners, but never such concerted opposition. His face paled but he bravely sought to continue.

Suddenly he heard a strident voice.

"Silence, ye spalpeens!" the voice roared. "Hold y'r tongues or I'll whip the everlastin' daylights out of iv'ry mother's son of ye!"

Peter Monk, whose presence William had not previously detected, slipped out into the aisle, took off his coat, rolled up his shirt-sleeves, made fists of his two big hands, and faced the hoodlums.

"Come on, me hearties!" he challenged. "Make another sound if ye will, an' ye'll taste the knuckles of me bare hands. Oi'm Oirish Peter from Dublin, the most two-fisted Oirishmaan in the Emerald Isle, an' me paws are fairly itchin' to connect with y'r wagglin' jaws."

Several of the lads made as if to accept the challenge but apparently thought better of it and sank back into their seats.

William smiled at Peter and then gave an equally warm smile to the hoodlums.

"We'll pause a few minutes," he announced, "so that anyone who desires to depart may do so. But I hope you'll all stay."

No one made a move to leave, so William launched into his sermon.

The message concluded, he extended an invitation for those who loved the Lord to come forward and make their declaration of faith. Irish Peter was the first one to leave his seat and go down to the amen corner. But he was not the only one. Five of the young men who had come to jeer came down to the penitent-form and were soon on their knees in prayer.

William explained to them what it meant to repent and freely accept the salvation of Jesus Christ. With tears in their eyes, the young toughs agreed that they were ready to follow the Master.

Peter clapped them on their backs in hearty commendation.

"Ye'll never regret the step," he exclaimed. "As fer me, this is the hoppiest night of me life."

As they left the tent Peter remarked to William, "I'll walk ye home, Muster Booth, if ye have no objection to the presence o' the likes o' me."

"I'll be glad to have your company," William assured him.

As they walked along Peter recounted the story of his life. Born in Dublin, he had depended upon his two hard fists to get everything that he wanted or needed. Finally, discovering that people would pay to see those fists in action, he became a professional boxer.

"But I can't go on with it now, Muster Booth," he told William. " 'Tis not the perfession fer a Christian. We fight in pubs or beer-halls, with everyone drinkin' an' carousin'. I had no objections before but now I can see that it's not a job fer a maan who's been saved by the grace of God."

"Is there anything else you can do?" William inquired.

"I'm hondy with hommer an' saw," Peter replied. "In faact, there's not owerly much I can't do. Never fear, I'll hov me more jobs than I can hondle."

From that time on Peter was a regular attendant at meetings, both those that were held out-of-doors and those which were conducted in the tent on Mile End Waste. Nor were there any further interruptions. If anyone so much as gave the appearance of contemplating trouble Peter Monk would unobtrusively slip over to a bench near him and reach out a hand to give him a warning.

The tent was not altogether satisfactory. It leaked in several places. During a severe storm it blew down. Vandals slit the canvas occasionally. But it served during the summer months. However, with the coming of autumn, tent meetings were given up. There was a steady downpour almost every evening, and the tent was cold and clammy. The only place available for an indoor meeting was a large dance hall, known as Professor Orson's Dancing Academy.

On the second floor above the hall a photographer, Jimmy Foggity, had a place of business, but he also occupied the "parlor" opening off the dancing floor. Mrs. Foggity had a desk in the parlor where she retouched photographs. It brought the Foggitys considerable business from the dance hall crowd but Mrs. Foggity, with an eye to additional appointments, also insisted upon working while William conducted his services.

The first service in the new location was held on Sunday evening, September third. It was preceded by an open air meeting at the Whitechapel end of New Road. In the afternoon William had preached on the street corner at the other end of New Road, and the evening meeting was preceded by an outdoor service on Mile End Road.

That Sunday evening and most Sabbath evenings thereafter William marched at the head of the column which he had gathered on the street corner.

Past brilliantly lighted public houses William would lead

his workers, all of them singing lustily. One of their marching songs was, "We're bound for the land of the pure and the holy."

Oftentimes people followed simply out of curiosity. Some of his followers would be decidedly under the influence of alcohol. William would not turn them away.

Some of the men loitering in front of the pubs openly jeered.

"I'll plant some stingers on their jaws," Peter suggested.

"No. We don't win people to the Kingdom that way," William reminded him.

Peter shook his head.

William had had the use of the tent without paying rent. Now he had to finance the rental of the dance hall. The rent was only twenty-one shillings a week but this taxed his finances to the limit.

Instead of taking offerings he had a box strategically located at a vantage point where people could toss in their coins as they left the hall.

On his third Sunday in this location, just when William was especially concerned to know whether or not sufficient funds would be available to continue, Peter sidled up to him.

"Look in the box, Muster Booth," Peter said. "A murracle's hoppened."

William glanced into the box. There was considerable copper there, a small amount of silver, but, gleaming part way down in the heap of coins, was the sheen of gold.

" 'Tis a sovereign, no less," Peter exclaimed exultingly.

William picked it up.

"It is that, indeed," he remarked. "Did you happen to see who dropped it in?"

"No, I didn't," Peter replied. " 'Twould be my guess that it would have to have been an angel."

"We probably don't mean the same thing when we speak of angels, Peter," William said, "but I agree that it must have been a messenger from God. Of that there can be no doubt."

Thereafter, for many months, there was always a gold sovereign in the offering box. William never discovered who the generous donor was. Occasionally he scrutinized his congregation carefully to ascertain, if he could, who the person might be. But no one was present at any of his meetings who looked prosperous enough to have been the giver.

The locale for the Sunday evening service was secure but William was still faced with the problem of finding meeting places for services during the week. It was his conviction that

83

"every outdoor service should, if possible, be connected with an indoor meeting, where, free from those dissipating influences which, more or less, always accompany outdoor preaching, especially in the streets of London, the Gospel could with greater clearness be set forth, further appeals could be made in favor of an immediate closing with Christ, prayer could be offered, and an opportunity secured for personal conversation with the people. . . . In this actual closing with Christ consists the only or chief ground of hope we have for sinners; without it, all mere resolutions and head knowledge will avail but little; therefore, we attach but little importance to instructing men's minds or arousing their feelings, *unless* they can be led to that belief in Christ which results in the new creation."

William was constantly confronted with major problems. Because people flocked out of the public houses to follow William and his band from their outdoor meeting places to the dancing academy, the police refused to allow them to march past these places of business. They had to take little-traveled streets.

There was also the constant struggle to secure funds for the meetings and the small amount which the Booth family needed to buy food and clothing and pay for their lodgings. Collections did not suffice at all. William had to get help from philanthropically minded people and this required careful preparation of reports.

"I'm two shillings short," he exclaimed one night when, in the wee small hours, he was struggling with his accounts.

"Come to bed now," Catherine urged. "Make a fresh start tomorrow and you'll find your error."

Stubbornly he retorted, "I must find it now. I'd toss all night long if I let it go."

It irked him immensely to be forced to call upon various groups and individuals for assistance, but when he received help he wanted to account for every penny.

He rented various premises for brief periods of time, a stable which was temporarily vacant, an old wool store. The occupancy of the stable was brief. The preaching and singing in their meetings disturbed the members of a gymnastic and sparring club which had adjacent premises.

But in June, 1866, the Mission secured the old wool store which was located at 3 Colts Lane, just off Cambridge Road in Bethnal Green. The room could only accommodate some one hundred and twenty people and the ceiling was so low that William had to stoop when he preached.

One phase of William's ministry brought him into special disrepute with the publicans in the neighborhood. He organized temperance bands, particularly among children. It was not at all uncommon at this time to see children not yet ten years of age reeling drunkenly along the sidewalks.

There were no laws regulating the sale of intoxicating beverages to children and many pub-keepers deliberately sought to make even the youngest ones slaves of the drinking habit. William lashed out against them in stirring language from the pulpit. He taught the children some temperance songs, among them one with the refrain:

> We'll throw down the bottle,
> And never drink again.

Publicans went into a rage as the little ones marched by their places of business singing this and other songs of similar import.

So successful were the young crusaders that the public houses began to lose their patronage. As a result the publicans appealed to the police and the latter again ordered William to choose different routes for his marches. Still the business of the publicans failed to return.

One evening, as William was walking home from a meeting, he was set upon by a crowd of hoodlums. Although he was tall and sufficiently robust to have defended himself against one or two ruffians, despite almost constant ill health, he could not cope with the dozen or more rowdies who swarmed over him. And, while he could have used his hands to good advantage to protect himself, he would never have closed them into fists. William was soon knocked off his feet. Several of the rowdies jumped on him and began kicking and gouging him. A knee in the groin doubled him up in pain.

But suddenly the pressure eased up. Like a whirling dervish someone whose face William could not see burst into the crowd and scattered them. There were groans as solid blows were rained upon the faces and chests of his assailants. Some of the blows doubtless landed beneath the belts of his adversaries. Then the tormentors who were still astride him were jerked to their feet, and immediately fled.

Sturdy hands lifted him to his feet.

"Irish Peter!" William exclaimed.

"I hope I wasn't breakin' up no private fight," Peter remarked apologetically, "but it looked like a free-fer-all and I thought you might be willin' to let me join in the fun."

"I'm glad you had a part in it," William admitted ruefully. "I was getting much the worst of it until you came along."

"Ye'd have handled them all right," Peter acknowledged, "if there hadn't been so many o' them. Did they hurt you sore?"

"I've a few lumps to show for it," William replied, getting shakily to his feet. "Who were they? Did you recognize any of them?"

"Probably hoodlums, hired by the publicans," Peter said. "You haven't helped their trade any, you know."

"I don't suppose I have," William said, "but I won't be happy until I put them all out of business."

"Then maybe I'd better just go along with you when ye're out fer a walk," Peter suggested.

"I can't impose upon you in that way," William replied, "and I can't possibly pay you for your services."

"Pay!" Peter snorted. "Don't talk of payin', maan. What ye've done for me already is something I could never pay for 'though I worked me fists to the bone, so don't ye talk o' payin' me."

"Well, thanks, Peter," William said shakily. "You probably saved my life. At the very least you kept me from getting a terrible beating. I'm most grateful."

"And now, Muster Booth, we'll start fer home."

"Don't say anything to Catherine about this," William adjured him.

"Mum's the word," Peter promised.

CHAPTER 9

During the next year William firmly established a reputation in the area. The work was just as uphill as ever but he became the best-known individual in the entire district, looked upon with considerable favor by many, hated and despised by those who profited by vice. He suffered no further personal attacks but Peter Monk, like an ever-watchful guardian angel, kept his eye out for potential troublemakers and no other hoodlums made bold to attack him.

One day in July of 1866 William was walking across the street from the Holywell Mount Chapel, a new Connexion church, just after trustees of the chapel had decided to close it permanently, due to the dwindling congregations which attended. The trustees were still discussing their situation outside the chapel after the meeting, dejected and unhappy about the decision which they had reached.

Mr. J. C. Moore, chairman of the board, caught sight of William as he was passing by. He began to pound his right fist against his left palm, and then pointed at William.

"*He* would fill the chapel," he said. "Let's have a conference with him."

The five trustees crossed the street and accosted William.

"Mr. Booth, your coming by must be the answer to our prayers. I cannot otherwise explain it," Mr. Moore said. "Can you spare us a minute? We'd like to discuss a proposal with you. My name is Moore. I'm chairman of the board of trustees of the chapel over the way. These gentlemen are my colleagues."

"I can give you only a minute," William said, "but what can you want with me?"

"Come into the chapel and we'll tell you about it."

William, mystified, crossed the street with the others, and entered the chapel with them.

After they were seated Mr. Moore came straight to the point.

"Just a half hour ago we passed a resolution which almost broke our hearts but which we considered altogether necessary," he explained. "Holywell Chapel is more than one hundred years old. It has had a long period of useful service in the cause of the Kingdom and in years past, before our people moved away from here, it was filled with worshipers every Sunday. But in recent years our congregations have fallen away. Our attendance last Sunday was . . . let me see. . . ."

"Just twenty-six," chimed in a Mr. George T. White, "and never more than thirty attend the services."

"We wondered, therefore," Mr. Moore continued, "if you would consider. . . ."

William jumped to the conclusion that they were going to ask him if he would be willing to entertain a call to serve as their minister and decided to nip the proposal in the bud.

"I'm sorry," he said abruptly, "but I couldn't consider it. I was a minister in the New Connexion, as you perhaps know, but I left that fellowship — which is your own — to go into mission work. I'm afraid that I couldn't possibly think of returning. I appreciate your interest but. . . ."

"Oh, we had no thought of that at all," Mr. Moore made haste to inform him. "What we had in mind . . . well, we know that you have found it difficult to obtain suitable premises for your services. It was our decision, made just this afternoon, to close the chapel; but when you came into sight it suddenly occurred to us that this might be the right place for you to carry on your work. You would not be the minister of our chapel. Instead, our chapel would become one of your meeting places and under your direction."

William glanced about him. Certainly this would be far better than the stables in which they had met before, better than the wool shed. But could he get people from off the streets to enter a chapel? Probably not if they merely hung out a sign announcing services, but what if they conducted street services first and then marched to the chapel?

"You're offering to rent me these premises?" he asked.

"Yes," Mr. Moore replied, "but I can assure you that the rent will be merely nominal. You can easily afford it. What would you say to sixty pounds a year?"

"For Sunday services only?"

"No. For services as often as you desire to hold them. We will vacate the premises. They will be yours to use as you see fit. And, while we can't make promises on behalf of all of our members, I suspect that most of us will want to join with you since our group will be disbanded."

William pondered the proposal for a moment. This was altogether providential, it seemed to him. He began to visualize the possibilities of services here. No cold loft. Comfortable pews instead of benches. *But they shouldn't be too comfortable.*

"I'll take your offer," he announced decisively. "I hope we can meet the rent."

"Actually, we're not greatly concerned about that," Mr. White replied. "We're not considering this from a business angle. We think of our chapel as a house which we dedicated to the work of the Lord. We'd like to see it put to good use for His sake."

"When you see the kind of people who will come here you may not be too happy about the decision," William warned him.

"As long as they are sinners who need to repent we'll be satisfied," Mr. White said with a smile.

"I can assure you that they will be sinners," William retorted, laughing. "This chapel will see more sinners in its pews than it has ever known before."

"Exactly what we had hoped for," Mr. Moore replied. "When would you like to hold your first service?"

"Is next Sunday too soon?"

"Not at all," Mr. Moore assured him. "The sooner the better. We'll have our final meeting next Sunday morning and announce the trustees' decision to the group. After Sunday noon the chapel will be yours."

William spoke to Peter Monk about the decision.

"Can you recruit some of the boys to distribute handbills? We want a crowd for our first service," he said.

"Gladly," Peter replied. "When do you want the lads?"

"Have them come to the chapel about five o'clock. I'll be there ready to give each one a supply. Then I'll start the open air meeting on the street in front of the chapel about seven, and we'll begin the service in the chapel at seven-thirty. How does that appeal to you?"

" 'Tis a foine idea. We'll show the Methodies how to hov a rale sarvice in their choppel," Peter said. "Can we fill it, think you?"

"We'll pray that they come," William replied.

Fortunately the weather on that July afternoon was favorable. There wasn't a cloud in the skies, nor a hint of rain, as the boys started out with their handbills.

"Give them a personal word of invitation, too," William suggested. "See how many each of you can bring back here."

William himself selected four boys to appear in front of the chapel with placards mounted on tall staves. "Service Tonight in Holywell Mount Chapel. 7:30 P.M. Come Early and Get a Seat," these cards advised. But when William began his service in the street he did so with only the four lads present to listen to his message.

In his deep voice he led out with a Gospel song, the others joining in with him. Soon a small crowd had gathered. William knelt down in the street to offer prayer. The boys muttered "Amens" at opportune moments. One or two shouted, "Praise the Lord." People stopped to gape at the spectacle. Some knelt in prayer.

William gave a brief talk on the need for repentance and ended with a personal invitation to stay for the service in the chapel. At about twenty minutes after seven his handbill distributors began to arrive. They had picked up small groups as they walked along. William continued preaching until half past seven and then advised the crowd that they could go into the chapel and continue the service there.

"Join with us," he advised. "This is not a Methodist service. It isn't an Anglican or Congregational service. We just intend to preach the Word of God."

A few hung back but when the majority of the crowd entered the chapel the rest followed. The doors were kept open so that late comers could walk in without feeling embarrassed.

William was not one to commit all his eggs to one basket. For this reason he continued the services in the other meeting places. The dancing academy was still available only for Sunday services, but they were held there weekly. Services at the old wool store continued nightly. Now he had another rallying point. The three made a triangle geographically, and William organized his people so that they called at all points within the triangle and for some distance outside of it to invite people to come to the nearest preaching center.

William established Sunday schools in two of these centers and had an excellent attendance at both. The open air meetings continued with most of them serving as preludes to the indoor services.

He conceived of his mission originally as offering a connecting link between the unchurched and the organized churches. He felt that if he could help the people find salvation they could then take their places in the churches. Years later he described his thinking on this matter in the following paragraphs:

"From the first I was strongly opposed to forming any separate organization. It was true that again and again the thought did come to me as to what could be accomplished for God and man by a people who were actuated by one simple purpose, and that was the immediate salvation of the masses and the entire devotion of those thus saved to the work of saving their fellows. The chief sorrow to me in connection with the sects in the past has ever been their divisions on the subject of practical godliness and immediate results, and with this in mind, I constantly put from me the thought of attempting the formation of such a people.

"My first idea was simply to get the people saved and send them to the churches. This proved at the outset impractical.

"First, they would not go when sent.

"Second, they were not wanted.

"And third, we wanted some of them, at least, for our own work to help us in the business of saving others.

"We were thus driven to providing for the converts ourselves."

Catherine was suffering once more from her recurring illnesses but when William discussed with her his plan to put to work the people who had been saved, she announced that she was going to aid him in this project.

"I can conduct classes for the women," she said. "At the outset I'd like to have Bible classes but I think it would also be much to the point to teach them to sew and cook. If they will make better homes their husbands won't run off to the pubs and their children will not be so prone to roam the streets."

"But you're a marvelous housekeeper, Kate, and yet I'm out roaming the streets every night," William remarked with a sly smile.

"I could wish that you would spend more time at home with us," Catherine said, "but I know that you must continue to go out into the highways and byways, seeking lost souls. I'm altogether resigned to that. But I must do more to help."

"That's a wonderful idea," William agreed. "We'll organize classes at once."

The project was so worthwhile that Catherine found recruits to assist her. These were women from other parts of London who needed channels for their energy which they were not able to find in their churches.

They collected clothing from friends and church societies and helped to renovate them for some of William's impoverished followers. With their interest aroused in the program of the mission, they were active especially during the closing months of 1866.

In November of that year a cholera epidemic broke out which was particularly virulent in the East End with its multitudes huddled together in shacks and sleazy tenements. Too, there was widespread unemployment.

"We must open soup kitchens," William announced to his family.

"You mean we'll have nothing but soup to eat?" Ballington remarked in dismay.

"Your father wants to locate these kitchens down in the area where we have our mission halls," Catherine explained, "since many of those people are going hungry."

Turning to William, she asked, "Will the government do nothing to relieve the distress of the people?"

"Governments aren't concerned about people's hunger," he replied. "They're concerned with votes. They leave the hungry to private charities. Do you suppose that your good women will help?"

"I'm sure they will," Catherine replied. "They are deeply interested and they're generous."

"Speak to them about the plan, will you, dear?"

"Of course."

The intolerable conditions of the area undoubtedly caused the London Evangelization Society to come to William's aid for the first time since he began his work. Their officers had maintained an interest in his program for many months but had never assisted him since they did not altogether approve of his methods of evangelism. Now they decided to accord him liberal support.

At the outset of his work at East End they had been suspicious of what they termed his flamboyant methods but they became convinced that the work he was doing was the most significant program being carried on in the area.

They decided not only to help with the welfare program but with the evangelistic work as well. With the closing of the Effingham Theater they agreed to rent those premises as the most suitable auditorium for the crowds who came to hear William preach.

William had probably been the first public character to coin the slogan, since quoted often by politicians and other persons in the public eye, "I don't care what they say about me as long as the newspapers say something — and as long as they spell my name properly."

It was in 1867 that William's name first appeared in the headlines of two widely different news sheets. The first, *The East London Observer*, in its issue of April 6, 1867, was decidedly uncomplimentary. It noted, after a brief explanation of who William was, that:

> This gentleman has for some time past occupied the Effingham Theater on Sunday evenings as a preaching place, and enormous audiences have been drawn to listen to his exordiums by the somewhat plagiaristic announcements of "Change of Performance" and "Wanted! 3,000 men to fill the Effingham Theater. The Rev. William Booth will preach in this theater on Sunday evening next!"

92

The result of so novel a promise as a change of performance, coupled with a formidable body of people marching down the Whitechapel Road singing, we are bound to say with not the most melodious of harmonies, no doubt drew many persons who might even now be ignorant of the exact kind of "performance" so vaguely shadowed forth by the bills. The boxes and stalls were filled with as idle and dissolute a set of characters as ever crossed a place of public resort.

From another point of view, much more favorable to and understanding of the service that William performed, the *Nonconformist* reporter wrote:

The labouring people and the roughs have it — much to their satisfaction — all to themselves. It is astonishing how quiet they are.

There is no one except a stray official to maintain order; yet there are nearly two thousand persons belonging to the lowest and least educated classes behaving in a manner which would reflect the highest credit upon the most respectable congregation that ever attended a regular place of worship.

"There is a better world, they say" was sung with intensity and vigour almost pathetic in the emphasis bestowed upon them. As they reluctantly resumed their seats a happier expression seemed to light up the broad area of pale and careworn features, which were turned with urgent, longing gaze towards the preacher.

Mr. Booth employed very simple language in his comments . . . frequently repeated the same sentence several times as if he was afraid his hearers would forget. It was curious to note the intense, almost painful degree of eagerness with which every sentence of the speaker was listened to. The crowd seemed fearful of losing even a word.

It was a wonderful influence, that possessed by the preacher over his hearers. Very unconventional in style, no doubt . . . but it did enable him to reach the hearts of hundreds of those for whom prison and the convicts' settlement have no terrors, of whom even the police stand in fear. . . . The preacher has to do with rough and ready minds upon which subtleties and refined discourse would be lost. . . . He implored them: first, to leave their sins; second, to leave them at once, that very night; and third, to come to Christ. Not a word was uttered by him that could be misconstrued; not a doctrine was propounded that was beyond the comprehension of those to whom it was addressed.

There was no sign of impatience during the sermon. There was too much dramatic action, too much anecdotal matter to admit of its being considered dull, and when it terminated scarcely a person left his seat, indeed some appeared to consider it too short, although the discourse had occupied fully an hour in its delivery.

A formidable letter appeared one morning in the mail. It bore the return address of Mr. Frederick Whittaker, Barrister,

Gray's Inn, and requested the presence of the Rev. and Mrs. William Booth at the earliest possible moment.

The family discussed it at length at the noon meal.

"Possibly someone died and left us a fortune," suggested the practical-minded Bramwell.

"Do you suppose that the publicans are going to bring suit against you?" Catherine inquired anxiously. "You have hurt their business considerably."

William brushed off these suggestions brusquely.

"No, no," he said. "Nothing of the sort. Mr. Whittaker is connected with the Christian Mission. He's their legal adviser."

"But why would he want to see you . . . I mean both of us . . . in his chambers?" Catherine inquired. "It sounds so very . . . well . . . official."

"That is the way lawyers always write," William retorted.

"Well, what do you suppose is his purpose in making this appointment?"

"There's only one way to ascertain it," William said.

"How?"

"By calling on the man to see what's on his mind," William said decisively.

That same afternoon Catherine, dressed in her best frock, and William, pressed and spotless, made their appearance at Gray's Inn.

There were a number of people waiting to see the barrister but his secretary ushered the Booths into the barrister's presence immediately upon their arrival. William had heard of Mr. Whittaker in connection with the work of the mission but had never met him.

The lawyer peered at the Booths over the top of his silver-rimmed spectacles.

"Ah . . . delighted to meet you. Heard much about you," Mr. Whittaker announced pontifically. "Doing a splendid work, I'm told. All reports of your labors . . . good."

William was impressed by the counselor's succinct manner and warmed by his words of praise.

"It is kind of you to say so," he replied.

"Not at all, not at all," the barrister returned. "You deserve all of the commendation that I have heard. Both of you. Now I suppose you are eager to know why I requested this interview, why I wanted both of you to come. Hmm?"

"Yes, we are," William acknowledged.

"Well, we'll get to the point," Mr. Whittaker asserted. "In

the first place, I want you to know that the Christian Mission board recently took action to form a special committee, of which I have the honor to be secretary, to relieve you of the heavy responsibility for obtaining pecuniary support for your work."

He glanced up over his glasses to see what William's reaction would be to this proposal. William's brow furrowed. He hastily turned over the suggestion in his mind. Finally he spoke.

"This is generous of the committee," he acknowledged, "but if it means that I thereby lose my independence of action I'm afraid that I can't accept the offer."

"It means nothing of the sort," Whittaker replied brusquely. "You will continue to be in complete and entire charge of the mission. We shall merely see to it that you are not troubled by the financial details of its operation. You would carry on exactly as you have done in the past."

"That is truly wonderful," William exclaimed, "but I have one more question. This arrangement will not preclude our taking offerings at our various services, will it? To omit an offering would be to cheapen our services in the eyes of our hearers and it would also keep them from learning the truth of our Lord's word that 'it is more blessed to give than to receive.'"

"By no means," Whittaker replied. "In fact, if you can report that you are receiving offerings from your people it will make the men and women of means to whom we would appeal more inclined to give."

"Well, then," William hastened to say, "it is decided. Please express to the members of your committee our sincere appreciation for their kindness and generosity."

"It's not kindness," Whittaker objected. "It gives us and our friends a sense of well-being to be able to make contributions to your worthy work. People of generous impulses are often victimized by unworthy causes. It is good to know of a cause as worthy as your own. And now to my second proposal. We are convinced that the mission should extend its services and branch out into other areas. We can secure the Assembly Rooms in Margate for a period of three weeks and we'd like to have services held there every Lord's Day for that period. In fact, we are ready to pay the rent for the premises if you agree."

"That would be wonderful," William acknowledged, "but I don't see how I can go. The services in the theater are better attended each succeeding Sabbath. But we have no one among our volunteers who could take them. We have people in training," he added, "but none are ready for such a responsibility."

"The committee had that in mind, but knew that we could secure someone who could speak for you, who would use your methods which are so successful, and one of whom you would thoroughly approve," Mr. Whittaker announced.

William was thoroughly mystified. The members of the Christian Mission committee all knew Peter Monk, to be sure, but Peter couldn't take such an assignment. Nor could he think of any other person.

"Whom would you suggest?" he asked.

Mr. Whittaker's face lighted with a mischievous expression.

"There's just one person whom I have in mind," he said. "We have had such excellent reports of this person's services that she is the only one we would consider. I refer, of course, to Mrs. Booth."

"Me?" Catherine asked incredulously. "Oh, no. I have had Bible study groups, of course, but they have been for women. These meetings should be attended by both men and women. I'm afraid that I. . . ."

"Don't be too hasty in making up your mind," Mr. Whittaker said. "We believe that a charming lady in the pulpit would attract people of both sexes. And you did it before."

"Oh, but that was in the provinces," Catherine objected.

"And people are the same in London as elsewhere," he reminded her.

"But I couldn't leave the children," she objected.

"Just for three evenings?" Mr. Whittaker inquired. "We shall gladly pay someone whom you would choose to look after them."

Catherine appealed to William with a glance.

"What would you say, dear?" she inquired.

"I think it's a capital idea," he replied. "And Mr. Whittaker is right. You are the one person who could do it."

"But I . . . I don't know what to say," she remarked helplessly. "I'd feel out of place in such a pulpit."

Reluctantly, however, she finally agreed to undertake the assignment.

The announcement that a woman was to preach in Margate occasioned a considerable furor in London. Ministers denounced the idea from their pulpits. Some few supported it. Before the meetings started the idea had been debated pro and con, serving quite naturally to build up a large potential hearing for Catherine.

"Unnatural!" some clergymen thundered.

"Christ has made all people of one blood. In Him there is neither Jew nor Gentile, Greek nor Barbarian, slave nor free, male nor female," others countered.

"Paul wisely decreed that women should be occupied with housewifely duties, but this woman has decided that she will usurp man's place in the pulpit," a Congregational minister announced. "Don't be led astray by this preacher in petticoats."

This announcement so intrigued Miss Jane Short that she decided she would like to hear the woman preacher and she was in the congregation when Catherine, pale and trembling, went into the pulpit.

William would have liked to attend the service but could not leave his own meeting at the Effingham Theater, but some of the board members of the Christian Mission did attend, eager to see how their experiment would work out.

Catherine was no pulpit thumper. Nor did she make any attempt to match William or other evangelists in forcefulness of speech. Instead, quite simply she launched into the story of Mary and Martha, pointing out that, as far back as New Testament times, Jesus reminded His hearers that women had different functions according to their capabilities. There were some Marthas whose places were obviously in the kitchen where they reigned supreme.

Catherine indicated that she loved her home and, had it not been for the importunities of the good friends who wanted her to undertake these services, that is where she would prefer to be. But, since her friends had insisted that she was needed for this special series of meetings, she had agreed to undertake them.

"But I shall hope to return to my duties as a wife and mother as soon as this brief period is over," she said. "In the meantime I shall try to open the Bible to you and from it discover God's plan of salvation for all — women and children as well as men. I can do it if I have your prayers."

Her obvious humility captured her congregation. She drew her examples of Christian living from the home. She told what it meant for a mother to gather her children about her and tell them the story of God's redemptive plan for the world. "There would be less children in trouble if there were more mothers who told their children about Christ's love for mankind, if more mothers taught their little ones the laws of God and helped them to see that these laws were for their welfare and were not barriers to happiness."

Jane Short had been a church member for many years but in this first meeting at Margate she discovered what it meant to yield herself heart and soul completely to her Saviour. She was the first to come forward to the penitent-form when Catherine extended the invitation. The second was Miss M. C. Billups, who had come to Margate with ambitions for a musical and literary career. Both of these young women made their professions of faith at the first meeting and regularly attended every service thereafter.

Catherine's talks — she herself would not dignify them by referring to them as sermons — were down to earth and practical. In considerable measure Catherine pleaded for the homes of London, for she saw the need to establish Christian homes as the primary objective of her mission. There is no record that the meetings continued beyond the allotted period of three Sundays, but she had made a beginning outside of the East London area, and she also drove the opening wedge into a vocation which had been regarded as the exclusive property of men.

One further result of her preaching, however, was the employment, soon after Catherine's services had terminated, of Mrs. Eliza Collingridge as Bible woman.

When Mrs. Collingridge came forward to the penitent-form and yielded her heart to Christ she felt that it was not enough.

"I want to do something for my Lord, Mr. Booth," she said. "What can I do for Him?"

"Take Him into your home," William advised. "Teach His precepts to your children. Win your husband to Christ."

"But I'm a widow-woman an' I have no children," she told him.

"Well, then, ah . . . seek out your neighbors, and show them the way to Christ."

"But I'm not very bright, Mr. Booth. Can't I take somethin' along with me to help me teach them?"

"Take your Bible with you," he advised. "It's the sword of the Spirit for every Christian."

Two nights later she was down in the penitent-form once more.

"You confessed your faith in the Lord just the other night,"

William said. "Why are you back here again? You haven't fallen from grace, have you?"

"No, sir. Thank the Lord!" she replied. "But I've been a-doin' what you told me an' readin' from the Scripters to poor souls, but they want Bibles for theirselves. An' I'm sure, Mr. Booth, that they need them. They're thirsty for more than I can give them in the short time I have to spend with them."

"I'll see about getting some Bibles for you," he promised.

He appealed to Mr. Whittaker.

"Yes, we can supply her with copies of the Scriptures, but I think that she should sell them — at least for a nominal sum — and not give them away," Mr. Whittaker remarked.

"Oh, I agree," William replied. "Giving the Bible away for nothing would serve to cheapen it in the eyes of its recipients. But the price she should charge for the Bibles should be low enough to make it possible for the poor to purchase copies."

"And Scripture portions, too . . . individual books of the Bible, that is . . ." Mr. Whittaker interjected.

"And Scripture portions," William agreed, adding, "for approximately cost."

Mr. Whittaker nodded.

"That can be arranged," he said.

Thus it came about that Eliza started on her mission, the first of a group of Bible women whom the mission employed.

"Oh, it's wonderful, Mr. Booth," Eliza told William a few evenings after she had set forth. "Already I've sold five copies of the Bible an' over a hundred copies o' Mark."

"Splendid," William enthused. "And you invite the people to come to our services?"

"O' course," she replied. "I've twelve of 'em who've promised to be here tonight."

Other Bible sellers were then employed. The mission branched out in every direction. Vacant stores and warehouses were rented. Some premises were exceedingly small, others would accommodate hundreds of people. For the next several years William found himself engaged in ever-expanding operations.

Limehouse saw the establishment of a branch where sailors and navvies, prostitutes and gamblers, came forward to the penitent-form to give their hearts to God.

Catherine busied herself in the preparation of a special mission to children which was immediately successful. The enlistment of children brought their parents to meetings. The entire East End of London increasingly felt the impact of the Christian Mission upon it.

William had in mind also the opening of outstations of the mission in other parts of the United Kingdom where he had preached in times past. One of the most successful outposts was the one established in Cardiff, Wales, where William had conducted a successful evangelistic program some years earlier.

CHAPTER 10

In 1878 William began toying with the idea of a change of name for the mission. This was occasioned in part by difficulties which had arisen between its members. There were now so many workers that William could not direct all of their activities personally, and yet all of them wanted individual conferences from time to time with the one whom they regarded as their chief. When he gave special authority to one of their numbers others among them protested.

"If we could only unite our forces so that our people would be willing to accept authority other than my own, I think we could solve the problem," he told Catherine.

"But you objected to the authority of others yourself when you were a member of the New Connexion," Catherine reminded him.

"I am aware of that," he replied. "I was young then. I wanted to work on my own responsibility and rejected the jurisdiction of the many who wanted to direct me in my labors."

"You think you would have been happier to have been responsible to a bishop?" she inquired innocently.

"No," he replied. "You know that I wouldn't have been satisfied with such an arrangement. I don't think that I would have made a very good Anglican."

"But how will you have authority without bishops or superintendents?"

"That's the problem," he admitted, "but authority of some kind is greatly needed."

"Then why couldn't you organize the work of the mission in the same way that an army is organized?" she inquired. "You could have leftenants, captains, majors and colonels in just the same way that the queen's forces are organized."

Peter Monk, who by this time was almost like a shadow to William, added, "And you should be our general . . . begging your pardon for makin' the suggestion."

William laughed.

"Oh, no," he protested. "That would never do. It sounds too ostentatious. I'd rather be a private in the ranks."

"But you can't be, William," Catherine reminded him. "You have to make the decisions for all of your workers. But if the mission were organized as an army you would have men serving under you who could make the lesser decisions for your workers."

"But there would be women, too," William added. "Don't forget our fine Bible women."

"Yes, women, too," Catherine acknowledged.

"'Tis a foine idea of the missus," Peter remarked. "Gen'ral . . . beggin' y'r pardon agin fer me presumption . . . I salute you as me commander."

He waved his hand in a simulated salute.

"You'd better stand up when you salute, Peter," William suggested, laughing. "That's military courtesy."

Peter stood, clicked his heels together, and executed an exaggerated salute.

"There. That's better," William acknowledged with mock sternness. "You may stand at ease, Private Monk."

"Well, now, William, you had better put on your thinking-cap and mull over the idea," Catherine announced.

That evening William followed her suggestion. He took pencil and paper and began to doodle. He first drew several figures who bore some slight resemblance to soldiers. One had a busby on his head, another the plumed hat of an admiral.

Then he wrote down several words.

"Hallelujah Army" were the first to be put down on paper.

He shook his head. The words sounded well, but they were too flamboyant for his taste.

Army . . . army . . . army . . .

The word kept repeating itself in his mind.

Well, why shouldn't there be an army? Joshua had an army and he wasn't a king.

Gideon assembled a band of men, actually a small army. Why shouldn't Christians have an army as well?

Almost guiltily he hummed the words of the hymn which Sabine Baring-Gould had written only a short time before — "Onward, Christian Soldiers." In William's estimation Baring-Gould was a worthy man. He was an Anglican, to be sure, but he was, after all, the rector of a small parish and not a bishop or archbishop — and William was exceedingly suspicious of such ecclesiastics. But the feeling of guilt was occasioned primarily by reason of the fact that Arthur Sullivan had provided the lyrics for the hymn and William could not abide anything that had to do with the theater. In his estimation the theater, next to the demon, rum, was the most powerful factor in the destruction of man's immortal soul. Yet William had to acknowledge to himself that the stirring notes of Sullivan's lyrics kept singing in his ears.

He began to hum softly,

"Like a mighty army moves the church of God:

Brothers, we are treading where the saints have trod."

He picked up his pencil and put down on paper the words:

"THE CHRISTIAN MISSION

is

A SALVATION ARMY."

A salvation army!

He liked the ring of the words. A salvation army! Why shouldn't dedicated people form an army for the Lord? True, there shouldn't be any salutes by which rank was indicated and acknowledged. There shouldn't be any courts-martial for soldiers who failed to carry out orders. But there should be uniforms with red piping to indicate the blood of the Lord Jesus Christ.

A salvation army!

The next day he communicated the results of his meditations to Peter Monk.

"How does it sound to you, Peter? Doesn't the name ring in your ears?"

"Aye, that it does," Peter acknowledged enthusiastically, "but why not call it, 'The Volunteer Army' instead? We'd all be volunteers."

"No, we would not be, Peter," William protested. "None of us are volunteers. We feel that we must do what we do. We must ever recognize the fact that we are always *on duty*."

"Aye," Peter admitted.

Later, at a conference with Mr. Whittaker, George Railton, James Dowdle and others, it was decided that a meeting of the Christian Mission should be called for Whitechapel for August 5, 6, 7, 1878.

"But this should be our last meeting as a mission," William said. "Thereafter we should be known as The Salvation Army."

Bramwell, who had already become a preacher of note, starting his work in his early teens, was also present. "If this is to be an army, Father," he remarked, "there should be one head to the organization. You should be designated as the general."

"Too pretentious a title!" William sniffed although, since Peter Monk had made the suggestion, he had undoubtedly been considering the idea.

"Now, really, Father, is it?" Bramwell retorted. "Is it anywhere nearly as pretentious as superintendent — which is your present title — or bishop, or archbishop?"

George Railton added, "I wouldn't be in favor of even using the army title if we didn't go all the way and have officers. If we proceed to organize an army in that way there should be a chain of command all the way from general to the humblest private in the ranks."

"But I'm not accustomed to giving orders," William protested. "You know that, George. Through all the years that the mission has been in existence I have merely suggested various tasks for our people, and always this has been in response to their requests for assignments. No, it's much too pretentious."

"It would be for anyone but you," James Dowdle replied stoutly. "I wouldn't want to serve under any other general than you."

Peter Monk grinned.

"See, Gen'ral, what did I tell ye? Ye're my gen'ral an' ye hov been all the time," he asserted.

George Railton intervened with a practical suggestion.

"We had better decide now what we intend to do at the meeting. You have opened the way already, Mr. Booth, by calling our attention to the fact that the Christian Mission is an army. Now we should adopt the name officially and call it by the designation which you have already applied, 'The Salvation Army.' I would like to propose that, since it is an army, you should be appointed the commanding general," he said.

William pondered the matter but Bramwell eagerly interrupted his cogitations.

"You had better agree, Father. This is what our people want," he asserted.

"It will make a tyrant out of me," William warned.

Peter Monk gave a huge laugh.

"Ye could try all yer life, Gen'ral," he said, "but ye could never make a tyrant out o' yerself. Ye wouldn't know how to act in that capocity."

"I'm not sure that I know how a general acts," William retorted.

"That won't be hard, Father," Bramwell reminded him. "You've been a wise general all through the years. A general doesn't act like a sub-leftenant, you know."

"That's right," William said, "and that's why I'd make a splendid leftenant."

George Railton glanced at the others in the group.

"It's agreed, isn't it?" he asked.

"Agreed," they chorused.

"I'm not sure . . ." William began.

"You're not the general yet, Mr. Booth," Railton said. "You're plain Mr. Booth. After the meeting we'll take your orders when we have elected you general. Right now the majority rules."

William accorded him a mock salute.

"Very well, sir," he agreed.

In the morning of August 5 the meeting of the Christian Mission was convened in Whitechapel. William made the opening statement.

"The Christian Mission," he said, "has assembled as a Congress to make war. It has organized a salvation army to carry the blessed message of Christ's crucifixion and resurrection, and the fire of the Holy Ghost into every corner of the world.

"Since our people have come from far and near in the United Kingdom to attend this meeting we can rightly say that this is our Pentecost. Do you not feel the power and presence of the Holy Ghost in our midst?"

It was a meeting where everyone gave vocal expression to their joy and satisfaction. Many shouted, "Praise the Lord!" Others lustily uttered their "Amens" after each prayer.

William had a feeling of exultation. These were his people, moved by an impulse to bring salvation to the people of the United Kingdom, and he felt that they would also be ready to go from the city, which he regarded as their Jerusalem, to all the world.

"During the year past," he announced, "we have had splendid reports from our outstations. This very afternoon we shall hear some of these reports from the fine workers who have sent them in or have come in person to make them. I have been greatly thrilled by them. I know that you will be also."

The first such report was made by Rachel Agar who had been one of the first to become active in the Mission and had acquired the sobriquet "Hallelujah Lass." At Felling, she reported, they had had four hundred and fifty come forward to profess their faith in Jesus Christ.

"The Salvation Army is on the march," she said.

There were similar reports from other workers, some from the environs of London, others from Newcastle, Cardiff, Birmingham, Southampton and Liverpool. Each one ended with the statement which Rachel made which became for them a refrain, "The Salvation Army is on the march."

There was one unhappy note which was struck during the course of the conference which was in contrast to the optimistic reports previously made. Some of the stations had gone deeply into debt.

"About this matter I must be very firm," William announced. "We do not have unlimited resources. I want you to know, first of all, that I receive no support myself from the mission. A few generous-minded individuals give me what our little family needs, but I receive no salary from the mission.

"Secondly, our good name depends upon our maintaining the respect of the people who from time to time rent premises to us or sell us goods. I must know in advance when you contemplate purchases or rentals for which you have no funds. I shall try to secure assistance as it is needed but I must know in advance what your needs are if our friends are to be asked to help."

The meeting was also the first in which a Salvation Army band appeared. It was not a particularly good musical organization but William was delighted with it.

One of the most significant actions approved at the meeting is recorded in the deed-poll which the delegates adopted. This would be known today as the articles of incorporation. It will be noted that, although the workers now considered the name, "Salvation Army," as the designation for the organization it was still regarded and described as the "Christian Mission." The deed-poll read as follows:

> The Christian Mission should be always thereafter under the oversight, direction and control of some one person who should be the General Superintendent.
>
> That William Booth should continue to be, for the term of his

natural life, the General Superintendent of the Christian Mission, unless he should resign.

That William Booth and every General Superintendent who should succeed him should have the power to appoint his successor to the office of General Superintendent, making a statement in writing, under seal, as to such successor or the means to be taken for the appointment of a successor.

That the General Superintendent should have power to expend all monies contributed, but should annually publish a balance sheet. That he should have power to acquire or dispose of property and to set up or revoke trusts.

No provision was made in these articles to amend them and, as a result, they could not be changed thereafter except by an Act of Parliament.

Years later Railton, summing up the feeling of those who attended the War Congress, wrote: "I do not believe when that Congress ended that there was an evangelist or delegate whose heart was not full of joy and satisfaction."

When all of the business had been transacted William announced that the Congress would adjourn to an all night prayer meeting.

The large company assembled believed in joyful, vociferous meetings. This prayer meeting was conducted along the lines of their beliefs. Prayers were interspersed with testimonies. But they had considerable competition. In the yard next door a large company of people had gathered, members of a butchers' organization. When the prayers began the butchers, somewhat the worse for a late evening spent in a near-by public house, began to pound on old lard tins with their cleavers. Others had horns which they blew lustily. Some playful members of the crowd lighted a fire near the ventilator, burning old hides and other substances. The Salvationists coughed and sneezed but earnestly continued praying. They were hardy souls, accustomed to overripe vegetables in their street meetings, inured to profanity, but imbued with a spirit which was able to take all obstacles in stride.

As soldiers in the Salvation Army they would face still more obstacles — hoots and jeers on the street corners, the sneers of journalists, the opposition of members of the clergy.

But they were ready to take all these in stride.

They were soldiers now, enlisted under the banner of the cross, in the ranks of a Salvation Army.

Within a year after this notable conference had been concluded they even had their own marching song, written to the tune, "Ring the Bell, Watchman," with words by Captain William J. Pearson of Bradford. He wrote and Salvationists sang:

Come join our Army, to battle we go,
Jesus will help us to conquer the foe;
Defending the right and opposing the wrong,
The Salvation Army is marching along!

Come join our Army and enter the field,
The sword of the Spirit with strong faith we wield,
Our armour is bright and our weapons are strong,
The Salvation Army is marching along.

Come join our Army, the foe must be driven,
To Jesus, our Captain, the world shall be given;
If hell should surround us we'll press through the throng,
The Salvation Army is marching along!

Come join our Army and do not delay,
The time for enlisting is passing away;
The battle is raging, but victory will come,
The Salvation Army is marching along.

Chorus:
Marching along,
We are marching along,
The Salvation Army is marching along;
Soldiers of Jesus, be valiant and strong —
The Salvation Army is marching along!

CHAPTER 11

The decision to organize the Christian Mission into a Salvation Army and to give William the title of "General" changed his status almost overnight. He had been well-nigh unknown up to this point. Few people were aware of what he had been doing in the East End and what his workers were accomplishing in other parts of England and Wales. But the happy thought that made an army of a Christian mission and a general of an evangelist brought him into immediate prominence.

He became almost at once a focus of national attention. There were those in the newspaper field who pointed the finger of scorn at him. *Punch* lampooned him. Many clergymen denounced him. Not yet had any considerable number of people espoused the cause of pacifism but the idea of an "army" of

Christian workers was repugnant to a host of earnest church people. He was called by various uncomplimentary names: religious charlatan, consummate hypocrite, a cunning scoundrel.

He chose a uniform for his Salvationists, a garb which both men and women could wear proudly, with a cap for the men and a bonnet for his women officers. He organized Salvation Army bands. They played in the streets and in the halls where meetings were held. He was criticized for marching, with the band preceding him, to a theater where he was to preach.

William had anticipated much of the criticism but when it came he shrank from it. Not so Bramwell, who by now was serving as aide-de-camp to his father. George Railton aided and abetted Bramwell. Whenever criticism appeared in the newspapers the two rejoiced. "Good advertising!" Bramwell would exclaim.

But much of the criticism was downright scurrilous. The Salvationists were accused of engaging in sexual immoralities. One rumor had it that the Salvationists frequently held meetings which they called, "Creeping for Jesus." It was alleged that the lights in the halls where they met were occasionally turned out and that men and women, on hands and knees, would crawl along the floor in the darkness. Thereafter the foulest obscenities would occur.

The very fact that the accusations were made was enough to damn William and his army. The origin of many of these rumors could be traced to the publicans. They suffered more than any other group in the loss of their trade, for the Salvation Army, more than any other organization in Britain, cut sharply into their clientele.

There was also criticism from some of the churches. The Army was charged with using methods of evangelism which were both vulgar and irreverent. This was deemed sufficiently important to answer and in 1881 the Army published a tract entitled, "All About the Salvation Army," in which answer was made in part as follows:

"Many of our methods are very different from the religious usage and social taste of respectable and refined people, which may make these measures appear vulgar, that is, in bad taste to them; but this does not make them wrong in the sight of God. . . . And, if it can be proved from the results that these methods lay hold of the ignorant and godless multitudes, compelling them to think about eternity and attend to their souls' salvation, we think they are proven thereby to be both lawful and expedient."

But the charges against the Army persisted and the Church of England in a meeting of the Upper House of Convocation of the Province of Canterbury on April 10, 1883, took action at the suggestion of the Bishop of Oxford. The bishop phrased his resolution tactfully, suggesting merely that inquiries should be instituted as to whether the results of the work of the Army were actually contrary to the aims and aspirations of the leaders of the organization.

It was a criticism of the rank and file of the Army but assumed the good faith of William, who was now called "The General," and members of his staff. If it had been directed against William himself he would, doubtless, have vouchsafed no reply.

"But," he exclaimed to Bramwell and Ballington, "when they criticize our soldiers I must defend them. Our people make mistakes. What soldier does not? I am certain that they are tactless in their utterances at times. I am aware of the fact that they are often over-zealous, but their hearts are right, their motives are pure. And I am convinced that not every cleric in the church measures up in ability, consecration, and tact to the vows that he made at his ordination."

"Write them a blistering letter, Father," urged Ballington with the impulsiveness of youth.

"No," William replied. "We want no controversy with the Church. The Church is our ally, not our enemy. Never forget that. Christ established the Church on earth, and it is His Church. All that I want to do is to set our good friends of the clergy right on what we are actually trying to accomplish, and what are our motives and methods."

Thus, in his own hand, the General wrote identical letters to both the Bishop of Oxford and the Archbishop of Canterbury, saying:

> I observe with great regret in this morning's journals a report of proceedings in Convocation yesterday, in the course of which a number of serious accusations against the Army appear to have been made. It seems to me very hard that the outrageous statements constantly made with regard to us should be credited without our having an opportunity to reply to them.
>
> There has been no change whatever in our Orders or methods during the last twelve months, and the only development I know of is in the increase, amounting to more than a doubling of the numbers, of those who are doing the work and enduring the sufferings to which attention was called in your Lordship's house twelve months ago.
>
> I am well aware that there have been of late a great many

efforts made both in England and in Switzerland to misrepresent both our teachings and our plans; but we have never yet met with a charge that can be maintained against us when fairly examined in daylight.

I enclose a note to his Lordship, the Bishop of Oxford, and trust that some opportunity will, at least, be given to us to meet the very grave accusations he appears to have brought against us, and which we venture to say cannot be supported by one solitary fact. There can be no doubt that such an accusation made in such a quarter will be used in such a way in the Press as to greatly increase the ill-usage of our poor people in the streets.

Our earnest desire to maintain friendly relationships with the authorities of the Church has not in the least degree changed. We might point with satisfaction to the enormous growth, not merely in the numbers of those connected with us, but of those belonging to all denominations, who in spite of the efforts of our enemies have been won to sympathize with us during the last six months. And we might in presence of these facts resign ourselves with indifference to any hostile expression of opinion.

But what I regret and would fain avert, if not too late, is a growth of a conviction amongst all these, that the scandalous reports circulated against us find ready credence with the authorities of the Church, and that the multitudes of poor labourers whose zealous efforts to diffuse religion cannot at any rate be denied, are looked upon no longer with sympathy, but rather with contempt by the clergy. I do not hesitate to say that the spread of such a conviction in these days when, as his Lordship the Bishop of Exeter has pointed out, the spiritual state of great masses of the population, especially in large towns, is so unsatisfactory, would be a national calamity.

Is it impossible for us to have an opportunity of meeting and refuting the groundless accusations made against us, which alone can account for the changed attitude of your Lordship's house towards us?

I am, my Lord, yours most respectfully,
William Booth.

There was further correspondence with the archbishop and then a meeting with him in which Commissioner Railton and two other Salvationists participated, which resulted in the following statement, written by Railton, which was given to the public.

His grace, the Archbishop, assured us that he never had any intention of making an accusation against the Army, still less of exciting public hostility to it, and that his words, used in the midst of a discussion in Convocation, must have been ill-chosen to have conveyed such an impression.

All he had meant to convey was that he strongly disapproved of the gathering together of young people at late and exciting meetings, inasmuch as there was great danger that, however excellent might be the intentions of those who held such meetings, young men and women, on leaving them without proper control might fall into immorality, as had doubtless been the case sometimes already.

George S. Railton

There were additional conversations with leading churchmen, among them Dr. Randall Davidson, later to become the Archbishop of Canterbury. Dr. Davidson had received many letters from individuals, both clergymen and laymen, criticizing the Army. Among the charges which came to his desk were the following:

> Mr. Booth is accustomed to adapt sardonically a certain text of Scripture, and say, "The last enemy that shall be destroyed is the parson." I cannot but think that a most awful responsibility is incurred by any who by their influence help on the propaganda of such sickening blasphemy. . . .

> Salvation Army processions consist of a lot of screaming, raving youths and girls, dancing and indulging in most unseemly contortions.

> Their proceedings can do no possible good, and merely afford an incessant subject for the scoffs and blasphemies of the publicans and their allies.

Dr. Davidson refused to accept the criticisms at face value. Instead, he made a personal investigation of the Army, the results of which were detailed in an article in *The Contemporary Review*, an excerpt from which reads as follows:

> Whatever be their errors in doctrine or in practice, I can only say that, after attending a large number of Meetings of different kinds in various parts of London, I thank God from my heart that He has raised up to proclaim His message of Salvation the men and women who are now guiding the Army's work, and whose power of appealing to the hearts of their hearers is a gift from the Lord Himself. I am sorry for the Christian teacher, be he cleric or layman, who has listened to such addresses as those given by "General" Booth, Mrs. Booth, and by some five or six, at least, of their "Staff Officers," who has not asked for help that he may speak his message with the like straightforward ability and earnest zeal.

It must be confessed that there were undoubtedly some Salvation Army officers who criticized the church. They singled out the church as an enemy. They portrayed the Army as the friend of sinners, eager for their salvation, and suggested that the churches were not interested in ordinary people. "Their concern is for the toffs with plenty of money," they would solemnly assert.

William made short shrift of any officers who thus arrayed

111

themselves against any church, Anglican or Nonconformist, but the Army was growing so rapidly that by this time he couldn't know all of his people. More and more he had to depend upon senior officers.

And the Army was expanding with tremendous rapidity. There were citadels in India where the uniform cap consisted of a turban instead of the cap worn in England. The Army was on the verge of establishing a beachhead in the United States and Canada, and the Booths' daughter Catherine was being groomed to set up headquarters in France. Branches of the Army were being established in Scotland and Ireland.

The Army was making such rapid progress that the purveyors of vice everywhere were up in arms. Those who profited by evil influenced the police of many cities so that the latter regularly arrested Salvation Army leaders and soldiers on trumped up charges. It made little difference that the disorders which accompanied the formation of corps in various cities were occasioned by brewers and publicans who saw the menace which the Army presented to their business.

In Basingstone, Hants, in 1881, the Salvationists were set upon by an armed mob which proceeded with clubs to break into the ranks of the marchers. The Army people made no attempt to defend themselves and were bowled over like ninepins. Instead of jailing their attackers the magistrates arrested the Salvation Army people and forbade them to hold further meetings on the grounds that they were disturbing the peace.

The Army officers and workers refused to be intimidated and when they persisted in marching through the streets they were charged by a detachment of Horse Artillery. Salvation Army people were threatened with personal violence or the destruction of their homes. Anyone suspected of sympathizing with the Army — whether or not he was enrolled as a member — could expect to have brickbats thrown through the windows of his home or place of business.

Rumors concerning the militaristic nature of the Army were so rife that the magistrates in Stamford appealed to the Home Secretary in October, 1881, asking what they should do if the Salvation Army opened fire on citizens or stormed public buildings in their borough. The propaganda spread. Some people barricaded their residences against possible invasion by this hostile army.

"How can they regard us in this light?" Ballington demanded of his father. "Can't they realize that we are an army of peace and good will, that our only weapons are those of the Spirit?"

"Never forget, son, that Jesus Himself was charged with 'stirring up the people,' and that the accusation was laid against Him that He intended to destroy the temple," William replied. "And He warned His disciples that men would spitefully use and persecute them. Both Paul and Peter were imprisoned for their faith. Why should we suffer less than they?"

William, being an Englishman, born and bred, had both a tremendous affection and great respect for the Church of England. He had been baptized by an Anglican priest. His father and mother had drifted into the Methodist church largely for convenience' sake and their son had gone into the Methodist ministry originally because of the emphasis which the Methodists had put on evangelism and because he felt at home in Methodist testimonial meetings and "love-feasts." But he never lost his reverence for the Church of England even though, at times, he became impatient with it.

However, he was greatly surprised when one of the leading canons of the Church of England, in the Lower House of Convocation at Canterbury, on Wednesday, May 10, 1882, suggested that many of the clergy were eager to attach the Salvation Army, which he called a "society," to the Church and use its members as instruments for reaching the masses which were as yet untouched by any Christian influence.

The canon further moved that the bishops should be invited to ascertain what the beliefs and practices of the Army were and to consider whether or not it would be possible to attach it to the Church. A committee consisting of Dr. Benson, Bishop of Truro, Dr. Lightfoot, Bishop of Durham, Canon Westcott and Canon Wilkinson was appointed to enter into negotiations with the General.

Bishop Benson and General Booth then began a series of talks in which others participated. Several obstacles to the proposed affiliation of the Salvation Army and the Church of England were immediately noted. The first had to do with the standing of the officers of the Salvation Army in the church. Few officers had been ordained to the ministry of any church. In fact, the very genius of the Army had been the way in which it had utilized the services of consecrated Christian laymen and women.

The second had to do with the ministry of the women. In the Salvation Army they were on a par with men. The church, on the other hand, did not ordain women to the ministry nor to positions as vestrymen.

There was also the question as to what should be done with General Booth himself. He had a unique position in the Army. Should he be dismissed from this position in order to place it directly under the authority of the bishops? Should he be ordained to the Episcopal clergy? If ordination were proposed to him, would he accept it? Or should he be given some advisory position without title? Bishop Benson felt, as a result of the conversations, that the Army was such a unique institution that it would be unfortunate if it were to be swallowed up by the Church of England, and he had serious doubts that ecclesiastical control would make for efficient operation. But he was still intrigued with the idea of such an army as the Salvationists in some affiliation with the church.

Thus, after exploring the possibilities of incorporating the Salvation Army into the church and reaching the conclusion that such would not be expedient, he posed the question to William, "What would you think, General, if we would organize a church army along somewhat the same lines as the Salvation Army but which would be under the jurisdiction of the church?"

"We would welcome the formation of such an army," the General heartily replied. "And we would be delighted to give to the officers of such an army any assistance within our power."

Later the General reported to his staff what the results of the conversations had been, explaining as he did so what his views were concerning the relationship of the Salvation Army to the church. "We must always remember," he said, "that we are not *a* church. Nor are we *the* Church. We must never be guilty of usurping the functions which properly belong to its different branches.

"It is for this reason, too, that I have never yielded to the importunities of some of our good workers who would like to have us adopt the sacraments of baptism and the Holy Eucharist. These, you see, are ordinances of the church. Many of our people, quite naturally, are members of particular churches. Some are Anglicans, others Methodists, Baptists, Presbyterians, Congregationalists and probably members of other sects. Whatever their church affiliations may be they should go to their own churches for communion. We must not take over sacraments or functions which are peculiar to the Christian ministry.

"You will remember that Paul makes a careful distinction between the various tasks to which Christians are called. Some, he said, are apostles, others teachers and elders. But among those whom he cites as servants of Christ and workers for the Kingdom are evangelists. That is where we fit in. That is our particular task.

"Therefore, too, I would hesitate to ally ourselves with one particular church, whether Church of England or Nonconformist. As Christians you may belong to some one or other denominational group, but the rank and file of our members come from many different backgrounds. I should not want to compel them to join a particular church in which they could not feel at home in order to remain in or join the Army. No, it must be our task to make a great Army for the Lord but to do so outside of any denominational group. Do you agree that this is the right decision?"

"I'm heartily in favor of your stand, General," George Railton replied. "You and I were New Connexionists. Certainly we would not want all of these people to be forced to join the New Connexion in order to serve in the Army."

"I also agree, Father," Bramwell said quietly, "and I pledge myself that so long as I'm alive I'll insist on that policy for the Army."

As a result of William's offer to assist in the formation of a church army and his willingness to share the experience of the Salvation Army with others, various groups were formed under Anglican auspices in different parts of England. At Richmond, Surrey, the Rev. Evan Hopkins, vicar of Holy Trinity Church, organized the Church Gospel Army. In Bristol Canon Atherton organized the Church Mission Army. At Richmond there was still another group.

The various organizations used the designation "Army," and songs which were similar to those which the Salvationists had incorporated in their book were sung at their meetings, and they adopted the exuberant type of preaching characteristic of the Salvation Army. The great difference between the Army and the various ecclesiastical groups was that the latter served under the parish clergymen and had no independence of action. Whenever a vicar disapproved of the program of the army unit which was established in his parish he was at liberty to disband it. But the majority of clergymen heartily approved of the program and the church army became a useful appendage of the established church.

A leading commentator of the period, W. T. Stead, summed up the service of the various church army groups by saying,

"The action of the Salvation Army has stimulated the social and evangelistic activity of all other churches. The church army honestly avows its genesis without concealment. Other bodies which have sprung quite as directly from a desire to emulate the success of the Salvationists are less candid; but acts are more eloquent than words. Even where there is no organized effort to adopt Salvation Army methods, the community, from bishops to policemen, have publicly acknowledged the influence of the Booths."

Despite its interest in and sponsorship of the church army, the Church of England never lost its concern for the work of the Salvation Army and frequently individual rectors would invite Salvation Army personnel in for special communion services. William encouraged his people to attend if they so desired. He clung tenaciously to his original proposal that the Army should not become a new Christian sect but was formed for an entirely different purpose.

The Army would not conduct communion services. The Army officers, even those who were ordained ministers of various churches, would not baptize converts. These were functions reserved for the church.

At the same time, however, the Army prepared a beautiful induction service, similar in some respects to a formal church service, for those who joined its ranks. It differed from a church service in that, while it was thoroughly Christian in character, it was not in any sense sacramental.

By the eighties the Booth children had grown into young manhood and womanhood. All of them naturally gravitated into the Army. William assumed, of course, that they would do so. It would have been inconceivable to him that any one of his brood would fail to take his place in the ranks; and it would have been impossible for any one of them to conceive that he would not do so.

Apparently all of them inherited their father's natural ability to lead. And all of them, save Bramwell, looked like their father. Bramwell resembled his mother in appearance.

More and more the General began to lean upon his children for assistance with the work. He was unaware of the fact, apparently, or too preoccupied to realize that Catherine's physical condition was gradually deteriorating. She had been a semi-invalid for such a long period that it had been taken for granted that she would never entirely recover from the long illness which she suffered.

Yet, uncomplainingly, she managed to keep the household going. It was much more of an army barracks than a normal home. They were no longer pressed for funds; now they were pressed for room.

Catherine didn't know from one day to the next who her guests would be for breakfast, luncheon, dinner or overnight. William was constantly organizing new groups and answering a voluminous correspondence.

CHAPTER 12

It was probably most natural that the first overseas branch of the Salvation Army should be established in the United States. The General had no intention of beginning such a movement overseas. In fact, he probably did not conceive of the Army as anything but an English or British institution.

However, some of his good soldiers emigrated to America and soon after they had arrived in the United States they determined to organize a corps. Elijah Cadman of Coventry, England, was the first Salvationist aside from General Booth to take a military title. Since he was in charge of the Coventry branch of the Army he assumed that he was its captain and he gave himself that title. Among the officers in the Coventry corps were Amos and Anna Shirley and their daughter, Eliza.

The three moved to Philadelphia in 1879 and determined to set up a branch of the Army there. As a corps headquarters they found a tumbledown structure at the corner of Sixth and Oxford Streets, Kensington, which had been used as a dispensary and store by the Union army during the Civil War.

When they rented this combined stable and warehouse most of the windows were out and the roof leaked. It was filled with debris but the rental was low and they decided to take it. Eliza Shirley urged her parents to join with her in establishing a corps there. When her parents protested that the building was scarcely one which the Salvation Army should use as a place for its meetings Eliza retorted, "Jesus was born in a stable! If that was good enough for Him this will do well for the birthplace of the Salvation Army in America."

The first service was held on Sunday, October 5, 1879, in

the building which had already received the nickname of "The Salvation Factory."

Pursuing good Salvation Army techniques, Eliza and her mother first held a parade and an outdoor meeting. A Philadelphia newspaper reported the event in these words:

"Two women, both good-looking, who were dressed in black, conducted their meeting, assisted by the male and other female members of the band. The two 'Hallelujah females,' heading the line, with faces towards it and walking backward, led the procession down German Town Road, singing a rousing hymn. . . . Crowds collected on every corner, and windows and doorways were filled with spectators while it moved along, followed by almost everything that had legs. Every bench in the factory was filled. Every foot of standing room was taken and the room literally packed."

When news of the success of the Philadelphia beginnings reached London it was decided that the Salvation Army would have to plant its roots on the North American continent immediately. George Railton was appointed as "commissioner" to North America, the first time the title was ever accorded an officer of the Army. In *The War Cry* for January 31, 1880, this notice appeared:

"News of the successful beginnings in America has come to us like a voice from Heaven and leaves us no choice. Mr. Railton must for a time postpone his North Wales expedition in order to take command of a force with which he hopes to sail about 13th February for New York, and the United States must, throughout their length and breadth, be overrun by Salvation desperadoes."

It was definitely not a happy choice of words, for "desperadoes" had an unpleasant connotation in the United States. Certainly no group of Christians had ever thus designated themselves before. Familiarity with Wild West literature and its bad men had imbued Americans with the picture of desperadoes as the wicked individuals who robbed stage coaches and gunned down good citizens in the streets.

Thus, when Commissioner Railton and his six "desperadoes," all of them women officers, landed in New York they were greeted as desperate characters.

The General himself had led the procession which, on February 14, 1880, marched from Whitechapel to the Fenchurch Street Station in London, accompanying the "desperadoes" on their way to embark for America. So many were in the procession that it had to be divided into two sections. It was brave with bands and pennons. William's long beard flew in the wind as he stepped out at the head of the procession. Hundreds lined the route of march.

"God bless you, George," William said, clasping Railton's hand in a warm farewell. "May your invasion bring great fruits for the Kingdom."

"I wish you could be with us, sir," George replied wistfully.

"Tell them I'll be over sometime soon," the General promised.

The weather during the crossing was such that Railton could not hold the open air deck meetings which he had anticipated but the captain permitted him to use the stair landing above the lounge. The Salvation Army band (consisting of only two instruments) played and George preached to those who occupied the lounge below. The passengers drank and played cards, seemingly paying little attention to the messages of the commissioner. But the tradition of the Army has always been to "testify" in whatever surroundings its members may be placed. And the result of these meetings was at least one convert who later became a candidate for service in the Army.

When Railton and his party landed at the Battery Point Pier on March 10 custom officials asked them what their mission was to be in the United States.

"We have come to organize the Salvation Army," declared Railton. "Ours is a peaceful invasion of your shores. We come in the name of the King of kings. We intend to preach Salvation in His precious name."

"Show us," one of the officials challenged, little expecting that Railton and his Salvationists would comply.

It was an invitation to service which could not be ignored. So the Salvationists and the single convert who had been made on shipboard held their first open air meeting in the United States.

George Railton planted one of their flags in the ground and, in the words which had been previously used by Christopher Columbus when he arrived at the beach of Santo Domingo, setting up there the standards of King Ferdinand and Queen Isabella, with a Salvationist difference, Railton announced, "I claim America for God."

But the official welcome to the City of New York was altogether different.

Having heard of the riots which occasionally accompanied Salvation Army meetings in England, the City Council had hastily drafted and passed an ordinance forbidding religious assemblies in the open air, except such as would be directed or presided over by duly ordained ministers or priests. It had been adopted, of course, for the sole purpose of halting any attempt to organize the Army in the United States.

There was no opportunity, therefore, to hold the outdoor meetings which were as necessary to the Army as the air which their officers breathed. After searching vainly for suitable premises in which indoor meetings could be held, George Railton decided on an exceedingly bold move, one which gave to his "invasion" the publicity which it needed to get under way. He prepared an *ultimatum* which he delivered, in company with his associates, to the mayor of the city. Copies of the ultimatum were also given to the newspapers and all of the metropolitan dailies were happy to print it. It read as follows:

The Salvation Army — America
Headquarters: 130 Liberty Street
New York

16th March 1880

To His Honour the Mayor and the Corporation of New York, I, G. S. Railton by the grace of God and by the appointment of William Booth, General of The Salvation Army, Commissioner for the various States and countries of North and South America, send greeting.

Whereas, under the authority granted to me I have appointed certain officers to carry on within this city such operations as may be necessary to cause those who are at present in rebellion against God to submit to Him, that they may be saved from sin and hell, and may be made righteous and happy in life, in death, and for ever.

And whereas it is an essential part of such operations that the people who habitually avoid entering places of worship should be followed in the public thoroughfares, and should, by means of services held there be made willing to attend meetings indoors. Which can only be accomplished by using everyone who places himself or herself under our direction to testify publicly for Christ, or, in other words, by making every Saul of today who is converted under our ministrations a Paul of tomorrow.

And whereas you, the Mayor of this city, refuse to grant permission to me or to anyone who is not an ordained minister of some religious denomination thus to speak in the public thoroughfares.

Now, therefore, I hereby most respectfully request and require in the name of the Lord God of Hosts that before six o'clock on the evening of Thursday next, the eighteenth day of March, 1880, an engagement be delivered to me at the above address from the government of this city to permit any person acting under my direction to proclaim salvation in the streets upon the same terms and conditions under which permission to do so would be granted to any other citizen whatsoever.

And I hereby further give you notice that failing the delivery of such an engagement before the above named time I shall forthwith remove the headquarters of this Army in America to some city where equal privileges are enjoyed by all citizens, ordained or not ordained, in the matter of serving the Lord and saving souls.

I shall do this with great reluctance, not being desirous to appear to slight a city where we have already experienced so much courtesy and kindness. But we must not fix our Headquarters where we could not develop in perfect liberty this line of action which, more than any other, has made and will make this Army a delivering force for the multitudes of drunkards and others who keep outside the range of all ordinary religious influences.

Despite the ultimatum the city council refused to grant permission to hold open air meetings and George Railton moved on to Philadelphia to work with the corps which had been established there.

William was overjoyed when he received a copy of the ultimatum, despite the fact that it was answered in the negative. The fact that the streets of New York could not be used by the Army for the proclamation of salvation did not dismay him.

"A stroke of genius!" he exclaimed to Bramwell. "It has the authentic ring of the Army."

"But did it accomplish any useful immediate purpose?" Bramwell asked dryly.

"Its immediate purpose? No," William acknowledged. "But Railton made his point. And he laid down the principle on which all of our work must be established. We must never appear to be suppliants, pleading for permission to proclaim Salvation. We're an integral unit in the Army of the Lord."

Railton's experience convinced William that it was time to open other overseas stations. His daughter Catherine was appointed to start a unit in France and William began to give her a special course of training for this purpose.

"It will not be an easy task, Kate," he reminded her. "We have no idea how the French people will accept the Army and what the French government will do. You know what opposition we have met here in England. There may be greater opposition in France."

"I've lived through it here, Papa," she said. "I assure you that I'm not afraid to face it there."

The General's eyes dimmed with unshed tears. Kate was a true daughter of a courageous mother. The regimen of their home had been Spartan and there were many times when his children resented the discipline which he and Catherine had exercised, but here was evidence that it had accomplished tangible results for the Lord.

Her training completed, on Sunday, March 13th, 1881, Catherine began services in a small hall located in the Rue d'Angoulème in one of the poorer sections of Paris. The reception accorded her and her small group of associates was not a happy one. Before long the neighbors petitioned the police to close the hall to their meetings.

The official attitude towards the Army (called *L'Armée du Salut* in France) was occasioned in part by the wave of anti-clericalism which was sweeping the country at this time. Somehow the rumor originated that the Army was being established in France for the purpose of restoring the Jesuits to power. Catherine had an uphill task for a period of years before she was able to gain a foothold.

Along with the commission to establish a corps in France was an assignment to begin work in Switzerland. Here, too, she encountered considerable opposition. Even in Geneva, with its long tradition of freedom of worship, she found the going hard.

News of the work of the Salvation Army was beginning to encircle the world. Small outposts were even set up in India. An assistant government commissioner named Frederick de Latour Tucker learned of these efforts and read of the work which the Salvation Army was doing in England, and became so interested in the movement that he began to emulate its program.

With a clerk from his office, who was also in government employ, he began to hold street meetings in Simla. When the authorities learned of his labors they reminded him that his work was scarcely compatible with his duties as an assistant commissioner. These were basically judicial in nature and the governor-general felt that it was incompatible with his duties as a judge, this being Tucker's essential function, to conduct services for those who might eventually be haled into his courtroom for violations of British law.

Under the circumstances Tucker felt it incumbent upon himself to resign his post and return to England. This he did and upon his arrival in London immediately set out to ascertain where Salvation Army services were held so that he could attend them. After the first service he sought out the General and presented himself as a candidate for a post in the organization.

"I don't recall ever seeing you in any of our meetings," the General remarked.

Already he had had a number of unfortunate experiences with people who, in the flush of the enthusiasm of a hastily made decision, had offered themselves as candidates for posts in the organization.

"There has been no opportunity," Frederick acknowledged. "I have only attended one of your meetings since I returned from India where I have been in government service, but I have held street meetings in Simla which have been conducted on the pattern of your meetings here."

"How did you learn of our work?"

"Someone sent me copies of *The War Cry*," Tucker replied, "and I learned enough about your program to try to make a beginning in India. My street meetings have, in consequence, been similar to Army meetings here. As a result, the commissioner told me that I would have to give up these meetings or leave the government service. Frankly, it was the only thing he could do. I chose the latter course, but I feel that I should learn more about the work of the Army before I attempt to set up its program in India. Nor do I want to set up an independent program, unrelated to the Army here. I'd like to do my work as a member of the Salvation Army of Great Britain."

The General shrewdly sought to appraise Tucker. As to external appearances he liked what he saw — the typical British public servant, but one who also possessed a keen interest in the people with whom he worked.

"Come and have dinner with us tonight," the General suggested.

"I'm afraid it would inconvenience Mrs. Booth," Tucker protested.

"Nonsense," the General retorted. "She always sets up extra places for unexpected guests."

That evening Tucker accompanied the General to his home. Tucker was young, personable — and a bachelor. At dinner that evening the General noted that Emma was immediately impressed by their guest.

Later that evening, as he and Catherine prepared to retire he remarked to his wife, "Our young man from India seems to have made a conquest."

"I noticed that," Catherine replied. "What do you know about him?"

"He came all the way from Simla to learn about the work

of the Army," William said. "He would like to establish an outpost in India."

"But what about his family? Who is he? Where is his home in this country? Where was he educated?"

"I didn't ask him."

"Oh, you men!" Catherine ejaculated. "You are so easily taken in."

"I'm a fairly good judge of human nature," he protested.

"No, you're not," she retorted. "You're an impossible idealist. You believe in everyone. You always take them at face value. You trust everyone."

"But no one can pull the wool over my eyes."

"Anyone can do it if they merely mention the word, 'Salvation.'"

"It's a good word."

"Of course it's a good word. But unless it is spoken in sincerity it has little meaning."

"Well, don't you worry. I'll put that young man through a course in Salvation Army tactics that will either make a soldier of him or send him back to India or Timbuktu," William promised.

The next day he had a long talk with young Tucker.

"You find our Army life appealing?" he asked innocently.

"I most certainly do," Tucker assured him fervently.

"Well, you've seen only one side of it," the General told him. "Go among my people and find the dark side as well as the bright. Call upon them in their homes. Find out where people come from and what they do."

Tucker accepted the challenge but before making the calls which William suggested set out, first of all, to visit his own personal friends. He fastened a red ribbon imprinted with the words, "Salvation Army," around his hat before he started forth on these calls.

William's second daughter, Emma, became interested in Tucker's preparations for his work and spent considerable time in his training. She was several years his senior but her interest ripened into love. Tucker was greatly attracted to her also but, after he had completed his training, returned to India with his status as a bachelor unimpaired.

After he had gone Emma was alternately listless and full of energy.

"What ails the girl?" William inquired of Catherine. "She has changed completely in the last few weeks."

124

"With all of your experience can't you detect it when a girl is in love?" Catherine dryly retorted.

"In love!" the General exploded. "Oh, no. With whom, pray tell?"

"With your protégé, of course," Catherine replied. "Didn't you notice the signs?"

"No, of course not," the General replied testily. "He didn't toy with her affections, did he?"

"Not at all," Catherine assured him. "His attitude was altogether circumspect, but that doesn't keep a girl from dreaming."

"A good young man," William said. "At least so I estimated him to be, but scarcely a romantic figure."

"So he appears to her to be. She sees him as a Salvationist in a white uniform with a pith helmet, riding on a white charger. She thinks of warm nights and sunny days, and pictures him in exotic India."

"Well, I never!" William ejaculated.

After Tucker reached India the General had frequent letters from him in which he told of his organization work and asked to be remembered to all members of the family. Emma also received occasional epistles from him, friendly in spirit and giving occasional glimpses of life in the country.

Finally one day Emma received a letter from Tucker in which he told of his marriage to a young woman whom he had known before he began his training.

"You would love her, Emma," he wrote. "She is completely dedicated to our cause. I wish that you could meet her and that she could have the privilege that I had of association with your dedicated family."

White-faced but dry-eyed, Emma showed the letter to her father.

"I was afraid that might happen, dear," he remarked. "You fell in love with him, didn't you?"

She nodded her head.

"But you're a good soldier, Emma," he said. "You'll take it like the Salvationist that you are."

Again she nodded in acquiescence.

CHAPTER 13

One morning Bramwell remarked to his father, "As I was coming back from my preaching appointment last night I saw men lying under some of the bridges that span the Thames. You'd think that the government would do something about that situation."

The General eyed him shrewdly.

"The government should," he remarked. "I grant you that. But what did *you* do?"

"I?" Bramwell retorted. "What could I do? I had no money to spare — barely enough for omnibus fare home — and if I had had any funds to give them those men would more than likely have spent them in a public house anyway."

"Ah, but the Master would have done something for them," the General said. "He would have walked down under those bridges and succored those poor fellows."

Bramwell shook his head. What did his father expect anyway? Did he conceive of the work of the Army as a kind of rescue operation for drunkards and prostitutes? However, while he resented his father's remarks, a seed had been planted in his soul.

He began to ponder a whole series of questions. Was it sufficient to try to save only the souls of men? How could they be saved when they were concerned primarily with a place to sleep, a decent place to go? How earnest a Christian would *he* be if he had to search in alleyways for food, if *he* had to sleep on a narrow ledge between the rushing Thames and a bridge abutment?

Bramwell tossed all night long, unable to sleep, as he pondered the suggestion which his father had made.

Was the General thinking straight? Was the plight of these men the concern of the Salvation Army? Wasn't the very genius of the Army that of evangelism, the preaching of Salvation? Bramwell lit a candle and opened his Bible to the gospels, a practice which his father had long followed. The words were reassuring. He found Jesus preaching in almost every chapter after the Master had begun His ministry. And this had been the commission on which the Army had been built.

126

Then he came to the story of the Master's feeding of four thousand, then five thousand. He found the Master ministering to women of the streets, and Jesus' missionary apostle, Paul, rescuing the demented slave girl from the evils of prostitution.

Was it enough merely to preach?

A few days later he had a conference with the General.

"Father," he said, "I think we should try to find a home for derelict men — a place where they can sleep and be fed, quarters away from the pubs where they won't be tempted to drown their troubles in liquor."

"We'll do it," said the General decisively.

"And Mother would also like to see a home established for young women who have gotten into trouble," Bramwell added.

"I know," William said. "She has often spoken to me about it. But we'd be criticized if we secured premises for that purpose."

"I'm sure that we would," acknowledged Bramwell. "Some people will insist that we thereby encourage promiscuity, that we make it easy to sin. In fact, some people will probably insinuate that we are establishing homes for children who are fathered by our own Salvation Army officers. But isn't it true that everything the Salvation Army has done has brought criticism on your head? When you insisted on commissioning women officers think of the furor which you created."

The General laughed.

"We'll go all the way," he said, "no matter how much we are criticized, no matter what people say. But before you establish the home for girls confer with your mother. However, don't load her down with any responsibility in connection with the home. Your mother is failing, Bramwell. She is not as strong as she used to be."

Tears sprang up in Bramwell's eyes.

"I know it, Father," he said, "but I'd like to give her a new interest in life. It may help her."

"It may indeed," the General agreed.

Bramwell immediately busied himself in seeking quarters for the men — sheds, warehouses, barns, places where cots might be set up and soup kitchens established. As soon as they were located, rented and prepared for occupancy, men came in throngs to the refuges. All of the facilities were manned by volunteers.

His mother was everjoyed at the prospect of establishing homes for pregnant, unmarried girls, and gave him her enthusiastic support. It was evident, however, that her enthusiasm for the project outdistanced her strength, for she tired quickly in conferences and did not have the strength to accomplish any of the actual work required in setting up the residences.

When the two projects were on firm footing the Salvation Army found itself the object of severe criticism as the General and Bramwell knew it would be. Clergymen suggested that General William Booth was encouraging idleness by feeding indigent men. Dowagers raised lorgnettes to their eyes in horror at the idea of caring for pregnant girls.

"Putting a premium on sin," they sniffed.

However, the two projects brought to the Army a new host of friends. Most of them were people whose membership was in many different churches and who had no thought of becoming Salvationists. Critical of their street preaching, they were, nevertheless, in favor of their social welfare program.

Bramwell immediately plunged into the task of securing funds to sustain the projects, aided by his mother. The General was impatient to get the program under way but was unaware of the complexity of the task. In the field of evangelism he could secure results as soon as a series of meetings was started, but it was much more difficult to raise funds for welfare projects than to win converts.

In the latter field he had only to go out on the street and begin preaching when a crowd would gather and, after a short service with rousing singing and martial music by a band he could certainly count on people coming forward to confess their faith in Jesus Christ. But winning the pocketbooks of people of wealth was altogether different. Here Bramwell, with his persuasive manner, showed considerable genius but the going was not easy.

People were not accustomed to give funds for relief except on the basis of immediate need. The average Christian would reach into his pocket for a shilling and give it to a beggar but to reach into one's purse for money to provide a shelter for the indigent which would be used at some future time and for meals which would not be consumed for many months was different. And the idea of renting premises for a retreat for expectant mothers whose children were to be born out of wedlock was altogether repugnant to a host of staid and respectable Christians. To them it savored of granting a reward for adultery.

"You've a long, hard job ahead of you, son," the General told Bramwell.

128

"I knew that it would be, Father," Bramwell replied. "I only hope that you're not disappointed."

"Of course I'm disappointed," the General retorted. "But I've always been disappointed — disappointed in results, disappointed when we were misunderstood by fellow Christians. But I have learned to expect this and live with it. We must forever set our goals high — and probably not reach them. But I'm determined that we shall make a start now and go on from that point. And you've given me an idea, son. Let's tell the people of London about the conditions of the poor. Maybe if we organize a movement..."

"What kind of movement, Father?"

"Well, for a long time now we have become accustomed to speak of Africa as 'the dark continent.' What if we set out to shock the people of England by speaking of this fair land as 'the dark country?' Maybe I should write a book on the subject. What would you think of such a title as 'In Darkest England and the Way Out'?"

"Oh, I say, that would be a shocker!"

"I should want it to be."

"A regular penny dreadful!"

"Good."

However, the General was unable to begin this project. Catherine's health, which had long been in a precarious state, steadily grew worse.

"We must get out of the city," the General informed Bramwell. "I don't like to move away but for the sake of your mother I believe we had better get a place in the country."

"Do that," Bramwell urged. "I'll stay on here but you and Mother can take a villa where it would be quiet and she could rest and relax."

Without further urging the General made inquiries in various real estate offices and found a cottage at Hadley Wood. Within a few days he made arrangements for the move.

"Do you like it, dear?" the General asked tenderly as they surveyed their new home from the front gate.

"Oh, William, I love it," she replied, "but how can we desert our people? Truly, it's wonderful. It's so quiet and peaceful, but I feel guilty — moving out to this lovely spot when there is so much that needs to be done in the city."

"We're not deserting our people. As soon as you are well enough we'll move back to the city but we'll keep this villa as our retreat so that it will always be available. In the meantime, plenty of fresh air, good food — we have a lovely vegetable garden, you'll note — and rest is on the agenda. Then my Kate will be fit as a fiddle."

The General hoped that he could spend some time at Hadley Wood but he received an urgent appeal to go to Holland to set up headquarters for the Army there.

"But I can't speak Dutch," he protested to Bramwell who had passed the invitation on to him. "Someone else had better go."

"Several of our people can," Bramwell replied. "Actually, realizing how precarious Mother's health is, one of the staff officers or I should go instead of you but the letter which came specifically requested your presence. Possibly you don't realize it, Father, but you have become a celebrity."

"Pshaw!" the General retorted.

Bramwell smiled. Since his father was getting older he sometimes felt left out of things. He knew that the General appreciated being wanted. It was a foregone conclusion that he would finally agree to go.

"I'll be a sight in bloomers and wooden shoes," the General remarked to Bramwell, "but I draw the line at smoking a long clay pipe."

Laughing, Bramwell replied, "Don't worry. We won't ask you to give up any of your principles. I promise you that you won't have to smoke. And it will do you good, Father, to get away. Don't worry about Mother while you're gone. We'll take care of her."

"I always leave her in the Lord's care," the General replied simply.

On the day when he planned to take ship for Holland, having purchased his ticket some time in advance, Catherine slipped in to London to consult a specialist. Although she said little about the state of her health she had been suffering greatly for a considerable period of time.

The physician to whom she had been referred was Sir James Paget, a famed Harley Street specialist.

After the doctor had given her a thorough examination he asked her, "Why didn't you come to see me months ago? You've had this trouble for a long while, haven't you?"

"Yes, for several years."

"With a great deal of pain much of the time? Isn't that true?"

"Yes, but it has been no more than I could bear."

130

"It has been much more than you should have borne," he retorted. "I'll be perfectly frank with you, Mrs. Booth, for you appear to be a person who can take bad news without fear. You have a malignant tumor. Unless it is removed immediately it will cause death."

"And if it is removed will I live?"

"I can't guarantee that. We don't know a great deal about cancer, what causes it, how to cure it. Sometimes, when we feel confident that we have removed all traces of malignancy, we find that it recurs elsewhere in the body. I can't promise that we can remove the seeds of cancer by an operation."

"Well," she said, "I'll consider it. But I don't believe that I'll have an operation. If I do I'll undoubtedly be bedfast for some months, won't I?"

"Yes."

"And if I don't have it there will be some suffering but I would be able to go on with my work?"

"Until there is so much involvement that you won't be able to do anything, Mrs. Booth," Sir James said. "We know so little about cancer that about all that we can do is to alleviate the pain when the malignancy has progressed as far as yours has."

"How much longer will I live?" she inquired. "I know that is putting it bluntly but I would appreciate a similar reply."

"Eighteen months to two years would be my conjecture, but that's just a guess."

"Thank you for being so frank," Catherine said. "I can plan the immediate future so much more intelligently — and perhaps the rest of my life. Now one more question — should I tell my husband?"

"If your roles had been reversed, if he had come to see me and I had told him what I've told you, what would you want him to do?"

Catherine smiled.

"That's a unique application of the Golden Rule," she remarked.

"Perhaps it is," the doctor replied, "but isn't God's rule applicable to all life situations?"

"Assuredly."

"Well, then, tell him."

"I will," she agreed resolutely.

The decision made, Catherine took a cab. On her way home she knelt on the floor of the vehicle.

"Dear Lord," she prayed, "give me courage to go on until

my summons comes, for there is much left for me to do for Thee. And be with William, Father. He will need Thy help so very much."

When the cab arrived at their villa Catherine found William awaiting her, nervous but eager. He jumped up from the steps where he had been seated and helped her alight. Her eyes filled with tears although she had intended to greet him with a smile.

"What did the doctor say?" the General inquired. Then he added hopefully, "Doctors are sometimes wrong, too. They don't always diagnose correctly."

"I'm sure that his diagnosis was accurate," she said. "He was frank and helpful."

"Yes? Well, what did he say?"

"We have never hidden anything from one another, dear," Catherine replied. "We have shared our joys and our sorrows, our hopes, our plans for the future. Now I'm going to share with you news which will come as a shock. I have cancer. The doctor feels that he should operate. Without an operation he insists that I can't live for more than two years."

The General's face turned white. He reached out a gnarled hand to take Catherine's in his own. He began to stroke it gently.

"Well, then, we'll have an operation," he said.

"It isn't a decision as easy to make as all that," she said. "He isn't certain that the operation will remove all traces of malignancy. He told me that it might do so but then again it might not. He believes that the malignancy has spread so far that it may involve other areas of my body as well."

William felt a crushing weight on his chest. If only *he* could be the one to face this malignancy!

Catherine continued.

"I prayed all the way home in the cab, dearest," she said, "and I received what I felt to be light from the Lord. I'm not in the least afraid of an operation but if I should have one I would be incapacitated for some time — just when we're getting our home for girls under way, and when Bramwell is making a good start on his home for men."

"They don't seem to be of much importance now," William remarked.

"They are important," she flashed back, "more important than ever. I want to see them completed while I'm still alive.

And now," she added practically, "if you're going to catch that boat for Holland you had best get ready."

"I'm not going to Holland," the General announced decisively. "I can't leave you now."

"Nonsense!" she retorted. "They want you over there to help lay foundations for a corps. Bramwell could probably do it but they wouldn't be satified unless you came. So let's get on with the packing."

"I can't go," returned the General dolefully.

Catherine gave him a stern glance.

"You're the General, remember. You accepted that rank," she said. "Now if you are to make the position count for something you will accept the responsibilities of your rank. It's up to you to get on with your job."

"You're a remarkable person, dear heart," the General replied. "Truly, in all the world there is no one like you."

"For that we should be truly thankful. But, for that matter, there is no one exactly like you either," she replied with a smile, "which is quite fortunate, for it would be a peculiar world if the population were made up of no human beings except slender William Booths."

The General broke into laughter but tears coursed down his cheeks. He took Catherine into his arms.

"These may be our last years together until we shall be forever united in eternity," he murmured to her, "but we'll make them the very best."

"All of our years have been best," she replied.

"Then these will be better than the best," he added.

The mere task of packing and folding clothing, placing toilet articles in his valise, and otherwise preparing for the short voyage helped to break the tension. It was with a more joyful heart, although still a heavy one, that he set out for Holland.

As the General faced his Dutch audience he gave no indication of the tremendous sorrow which pressed down upon his heart. Yet he preached with all of his old fire to the combined Dutch and English congregation but he felt as if he were preaching in a dream.

His friends in Holland wanted him to remain with them for at least a month but he explained why this would be impossible and, having made a brave start, he left the meetings to others.

"You can do as well — or better — than I can," he said.

"Every word that I utter comes in an alien tongue and has to be communicated to the people through the medium of an interpreter. They came to hear me because I was a new voice. But you speak to them in their mother tongue. I know that I shall hear good reports of your work."

Monday evening he caught the late boat home.

But after he landed on Tuesday morning it seemed hours before he could reach Catherine's side. As soon as he entered the house he held her close, his long arms enfolding her.

"You're all right, precious?" he murmured.

"Of course I'm all right," she said.

"I was afraid. . . ."

"We must not be," she reminded him. "We must continue to work as if I were to be with you for many years. Remember, dear, that we face what we call death daily. You may be taken before I am, in the providence of God. But we are going to continue with our work as if we were in the presence of death all the time, but also as if we were destined to live for decades beyond these present years. And we must both keep in mind that the Lord has assured us that we can never die, that we are always in the presence of life. When my earthly days are concluded I shall only step over the threshold into everlasting life. You believe that, do you not, dear heart?"

"Yes, I do believe," he replied fervently.

"Well, then, if we both believe that to be true let us demonstrate our faith by the way we live, whether our days on this earth are few or many. I am going on with my work, and I want you to do so also."

William sensed that, while Catherine was willing to share the unfortunate tidings with him, she did not want to divulge it to their children. However, unbeknown to Catherine, the General held a family conference.

"What I am revealing to you," he said to his children, "I do not want you to divulge to your mother. I can't ask you to show her more consideration than you do for you are truly precious children and you have always accorded both your mother and me unswerving loyalty such as few parents receive from their children.

"But Mother has been to the doctor and he has informed her that she has cancer and that in a matter of months — probably within the next eighteen — she will leave us. We must make these months the happiest in her life. And the way for you to do it will be never to let on by word or deed that you are aware of her condition. Be your happy selves. I know that I am asking a great deal of you but I know that we can do it."

"I'll take over the responsibility for completing plans for her home for girls," Bramwell promised.

"Take the major part of it but leave something for her to do," the General replied.

"I could take some of her speaking assignments," Emma offered.

"I'd be glad to serve in that capacity, too," Eva volunteered.

"Very well, but only when she doesn't seem fit to handle them herself. She should continue her normal, busy life for as long as possible. One more matter — ever since our honeymoon on the Isle of Wight she has expressed her love for the sea, her desire to live some day within sight of it. I can rent a lovely little cottage at Clacton. What would you think if we moved there? Most of you had better stay in the city, but all of you should make a practice of dropping in at least once a week if we move there. Shall we do it?"

"Let me go down there, too, Father," Eva volunteered. "Let Emma do the preaching for mother."

"Excellent," the General agreed, "but now for an excuse to make the move."

"How's *your* health, Father?" Bramwell inquired solicitously.

"My health? Why, Bramwell, you know that it has never been better."

"It seemed to me the other day that I detected a racking cough," Bramwell suggested innocently.

"Nonsense!" the General testily retorted.

"Are you certain, Father?" Bramwell asked, an expression of mock concern on his pudgy countenance.

"Positive."

"But, Father, you could begin to feel poorly, couldn't you? Suppose we should move down there for your sake," Bramwell suggested. "Emma and I could suggest to Mother that we thought that the sea air would do you worlds of good, keep you from over-taxing yourself, make it possible for you to get more rest."

The General caught the point.

"You devious rascal!" he exclaimed. "Very well. The two of you conspirators can see her at once. But, mind you, you're suggesting it for my sake — not for hers."

"Trust us," promised Emma.

This, then, was what they did.

Catherine fell in with their plans immediately.

Since the General had always had bronchial trouble and coughing spells it required no special acting on the General's part to appear ill enough to necessitate a change of climate but he did an excellent job of pretending that he opposed the move.

"I'd be too far away from the scene of action," he protested to his children in Catherine's presence.

"But, Father, Bramwell could take care of everything for you, and we'd run down to confer with you every few days," Eva suggested.

Weakly Catherine joined in the conversation.

"It would be wise to follow their suggestion," she remarked, "and I think that the sea air would be good for me, too."

"We-ell, then, perhaps we should do that," the General grudgingly agreed. "We could try it for a few months at least, and see if I benefit from it."

"You've always said that you wanted to write the story of the Army," Bramwell said. "Couldn't you take the time now to get it down on paper? Now that George Railton's back from America he will help me at headquarters, and the girls will help."

Thus it was decided. Catherine, aware of the sentence of death hanging over her head, could yet forget about it in what she felt was a ministry to her husband's needs.

The General felt himself inadequate to the task of writing a journal of the Army and a brilliant journalist, Mr. W. T. Stead, was invited to assist him in the project.

In the meantime the headquarters staff went ahead to implement William Booth's plans for the poor. It was decided that, although food was needed by the impoverished people of London, if it were given away it would keep people from making any attempt to provide for themselves. They would become, in effect, "rice Christians." Therefore, the Army would sell both bread and potatoes to people in need as long as they could pay for it. It would be given to those who were out of funds. Food depots were opened and were soon visited by crowds of people.

William Booth's journal, written and published piecemeal, came with tremendous impact upon the citizens of Great Britain. One paragraph was commented upon both in the newspapers and in the Houses of Parliament. It set up what became known as "The Standard of the London Cab-Horse." The General, aided by Mr. Stead, had written:

"When in the streets of London a Cab-Horse, weary or careless or stupid, trips and falls and lies stretched out in the midst of traffic, there is no question of debating how he came to stumble before we try to get him on his legs again.

"The Cab-Horse is a very real illustration of poor broken-down humanity; he usually falls down because of overwork and underfeeding. . . . It may have been due to these causes, or it may have been all his own fault that he has broken his knees and smashed the shafts, but that does not matter. If not for his own sake, then merely in order to prevent an obstruction of the traffic, all attention is concentrated upon the question of how we are to get him on his legs again. . . . Every Cab-Horse in London has three things — a shelter for the night, food for its stomach, and work allotted to it by which it can earn its corn.

"These are the two points in the Cab-Horse's charter. When he is down he is helped up, and while he lives he has food, shelter and work."

"That is a great simile, General," Mr. Stead suggested. "We treat our cab-horses better than we treat men. We are more concerned about a fallen steed than we are about a fallen man. We'll prick the consciences of the people of England with this story. But is it enough merely to point out what conditions are without offering a program for their amelioration?"

"By no manner of means," the General replied. "Haven't I told you my plan for colonies?"

"Colonies? No, I don't believe that you have. Surely you don't mean to do with the poor what we did early in the century with criminals — find some new Australia and ship them out to it?"

"No. Certainly not," the General replied. "But there is something to be said in favor of that scheme since the children of those convicts who were sent to the colonies have actually become respectable, courageous and useful citizens — at least, so I have been told."

"Then what are your colonies to be?"

"As a matter of fact, only one of these groups would actually be a true colony. I'm just using that term for want of a better one. But I think that there should be in every city a place of refuge to which people could go for food, clothing, shelter, a bed at night, and the touch of a friendly hand. I'd call that my city colony. We are working on that right now — at least Bramwell is occupied with it — and George Railton is helping him.

"We would call our second group the farm colony. It would be established especially for men who are so plagued with the drink habit that they can't escape if we keep them in the city. But we would rent several vacant farms, send them there — voluntarily, of course — and let them get fresh air, good food, milk instead of liquor."

"It would seem to me that this would encourage idleness. Wouldn't men elect to go to the country for a pleasant vacation?" Mr. Stead inquired.

"You might describe it as a vacation," the General replied, "but we would put men to work, light labor at first, heavier after their muscles have become accustomed to it. And they would be paid for their efforts, but have no opportunity to spend their money for drink."

"A capital idea," Mr. Stead remarked.

"But we have in mind still another colony," the General added, "and this might well be conceived of as a true colony. There are some people in the cities who could never escape from the sordid conditions which surround them. But suppose that we open up tracts of land overseas — in Canada, West Australia, South Africa and other similar areas. We would pay for the cost of transportation — I'm sure that the steamship lines would co-operate — and pay their way out to those colonies. We would arrange to find jobs for them when they arrived at their destinations. Eventually they might save up their money and become farmers themselves — or at least establish themselves in some useful form of labor.

"The Irish, for instance, have emigrated in successive waves both to the colonies and to the United States, as the result of potato famines. Most of them have been country folk but some have come from the cities. But we would take city people, whole families, and help to establish them overseas. How does that appeal to you?"

"Excellent! Excellent!" exclaimed Mr. Stead. "Let me put it in the book."

"Do so by all means."

Conferences with Mr. Stead and the writing of the book provided the General with a means of escape from the sorrow which was now encompassing him. Catherine's sufferings were

138

becoming greater and greater. Even sedatives failed to provide relief from the excruciating pain which she suffered.

William, assisted by Eva, provided the constant care which Mrs. Booth needed but it was painfully evident that her earthly life was nearing its end. But during every interval in which, for a time, the pain abated, Catherine's every thought was for the Army and her family. As a good soldier she could not seem to relinquish her duties or lay them aside even for a moment.

One event occurred at the time which helped Catherine bear up and which kept the family in a turmoil, the kind of disorder which can only occur when preparations are being made for a wedding.

Frederick Tucker had returned from India. Soon after his marriage his lovely bride of only a few months had died and, after waiting for several years, apparently he had returned to England for two purposes. The first had to do with his work. His labors in India had borne fruit but problems had arisen which he felt should be referred to the General.

His second purpose was personal. He had been unable to forget the General's daughter who had given so many hours of her time to his training, the gentle, warm-hearted, self-effacing Emma. He had regarded her as an elder sister during his training period, but now there was a different feeling in his heart for her.

"I should have asked this question years ago," he told her, "but it was only when our correspondence broke off that I knew that of which my heart had been aware all the time — that I loved you. Now I can ask the question. Emma dear, will you marry me? Will you go out to India with me and help to establish the Army there? I need you greatly, but India needs you even more than I do."

"My heart has always been with you, darling," Emma replied. "When you went to India a few years ago the greater part of me went with you."

So a wedding was planned.

The groom wore the robes of the country of his adoption. These robes had also become the uniform of the Army in the sub-continent. He was barefooted, and the Indian sun had colored his skin sufficiently to have made him appear to be Indian-born. Only his blue eyes and fair hair proclaimed the land of his birth as England.

Never one to miss an opportunity to take up a collection,

the General made a plea for the foreign work of the Army midway through the ceremony, and more than five thousand pounds were subscribed.

"Take it with you, my boy," the General said to Tucker. "It will help you get the work started in the land of your adoption."

"Salvation for the people of India! I wish I were young enough to stand in your shoes," Catherine whispered to Emma. "May God go with you, dearest daughter!"

"But I'll be barefooted from now on, Mother," Emma remarked tenderly, "and I know that you'll be standing beside us in all of our labors."

"I will. I will," uttered Catherine fervently.

CHAPTER 14

Catherine's ailment was an incurable breast cancer. She finally agreed to an operation which was performed by Sir James, but after it was completed he told the family that the involvement was such that it was merely a matter of time before Catherine would die. After the operation the wound continued to suppurate and the agonies which she suffered were indescribable.

Again and again, when death seemed imminent, the family was summoned to her bedside, but each time she would rally and her pulse would become stronger.

"According to all of the principles of medical science she should not be alive now," Sir James told the General. "I can't understand what keeps her going."

"I imagine that it must be the prayers of our family and the many thousands of people whose lives she has blessed," William replied.

Although, because of her sufferings, Catherine prayed constantly that death might come soon, she continued to live. At times the General could be found at night kneeling beside her bed and praying for her recovery. On other occasions he would repair to his study and walk the floor until dawn.

One night he made an entry in his diary in which he said:

"I am sixty years old, and for the first time during all these long years, so far as memory serves me, has God, in infinite

140

mercy, allowed me to have any sorrow that I could not cast on Him."

Under another date there was the following entry:

"By the time the children had gone she was completely worn out, and I resolved to have the remainder of the night alone with her. What passed that night can never be revealed. It will never be half remembered by myself until the day of Eternity dawns. It was a renewal, in all of its tenderness and sweetness and a part of its very ecstasy of our first love. It seemed, I believe to us both, in spite of all the painful circumstances of the hour, a repetition of some of those blissful hours we spent together in the days of our betrothal. Oh, the wonderful things!

"I wept, prayed, and believed, and exulted. We were in Jordan as it were together. Evidently she could not bear to let me go from her bedside or loose my hand. She had come back, she said, to her first love. I saw how exhausted she was, and again and again entreated her to consider her poor body and try to get a little sleep; and when I made as though I would leave her she upbraided me in the gentlest, most expressive, and most effectual manner, by saying, 'Can you not watch with me one night? It will soon be over, and what matters a few hours shorter or longer now? I have done with the body. I shall soon leave it forever.'

"And so we watched and counseled and prayed and believed together through that long night."

There was one other entry which William made in the book shortly before the end came. He wrote:

"She took hold of my hand almost at the very beginning of the night, and took the ring off her finger and, slipping it onto mine, said: 'By this token we were united for time, and by it we are united for eternity.' I kissed her, and promised that I would be faithful to the vow and be hers and hers alone for ever and ever."

Catherine died a few days later, early in the morning of the fourth of October, 1890. Only William was present during her final moments. Later hundreds of people passed by her bier as her body lay in state in the Salvation Army citadel. Her funeral was such as is rarely accorded royalty, for thousands of people from all walks of life were present.

Much against William's inclination the funeral and the procession which followed became a veritable Salvation Army pageant. William discovered that one of the prices paid for the acquisition of the rank of "General" was that a person thereby lost the right to private grief as well as private joy.

The funeral over, William plunged immediately into the work which had piled up during the period of her illness. The General's "Darkest England" program was running into difficulties.

Leader of the opposition was Professor Thomas Huxley. He was one of the most honored scientists of the time; and the intellectuals of the period regarded science as the touchstone of all learning. Huxley despised the Church, but he regarded the Salvation Army with even greater contempt. To his mind it was a foul excrescence, a parasite attached to another noxious growth, a cancer feeding upon a cancer.

Having viewed the ornate flag of the Army in one of their parades, having listened to the Army's brass bands, and heard their hymns — many of which were parodies of the popular songs of the day — there was nothing good that he could say about the Army. With loathing and contempt he described the creed and practice of the Army as "Corybantic Christianity."

He regarded William Booth as a liar and a rogue and "In Darkest England" as a most perilous and fanatical conspiracy which threatened the stability of the realm and placed the crown in jeopardy.

He took this stand even though Queen Victoria had expressed her approval of the program and though it also had the blessing of leading Anglican clergymen and the Roman Catholic Cardinal Manning. Mr. Huxley posed the question to "prudent men and good citizens whether they ought to aid in the establishment of an organization which, under sundry, by no means improbable contingencies, may easily become a worse and more dangerous nuisance than the mendicant friars of the Middle Ages."

Huxley revived the myth that the Salvation Army was both a military and political menace to the life and welfare of the people of Great Britain, the same charge which had previously been made in America when the Army sought to begin its work there. Mr. Huxley accused the General of seeking to establish socialism, warning against "despotic socialism in all its forms and more particularly in its Boothian disguise."

"He and his friends don't seem to realize that we're actually erecting a bulwark against socialism," the General exclaimed to Bramwell. "We want to find work for people to do under our present form of government, using all of the means for doing so that we can find in a capitalist society."

"Who are our chief critics in addition to Mr. Huxley?" Bramwell inquired.

"They are an interesting coalition," the General replied. "Mr. C. S. Loch of the Charity Organization Society is one of them. He evidently feels that the Army is seeking to usurp the functions of his group whereas there is room for the Army, his society, and many more benevolent groups to cope with the problems of poverty, drunkenness and crime. I suspect that Mr. Huxley is our bitterest foe, but he is joined by churchmen also. Strange bedfellows, indeed!"

"But it does seem an impossible scheme," Bramwell remarked. "After all, our Army is comparatively small. We're scarcely equipped to undertake a program which would become worldwide in scope."

"Gideon's army was also small but it defeated the Midianites," the General reminded him. "Should we hesitate to undertake the project merely because it is large enough to provide us a stirring challenge?"

"No, but. . . ."

Dryly the General remarked, "I suspect that some of the disciples felt the same way about Jesus' idea of a Kingdom of God on earth."

Bramwell retorted, "Remember, Father, that that was proposed eighteen centuries ago and the Kingdom still hasn't been established."

"That's only partially true," the General said. "Assuredly not everyone now living is in the Kingdom, but think of its scope. And the fact that the Kingdom has not enlisted everyone doesn't make me any the less zealous for it. Bramwell, let's never join with our critics and say that, because a program is difficult to establish, we should give it up."

"We won't, Father," Bramwell assured him.

However, unknown to the General, Bramwell had several meetings with the ever enlarging staff at International Headquarters, including Evangeline, the only one of the General's daughters who was still resident in England.

"Father will wear himself out," Bramwell explained. "He has to concern himself not only with the task of setting up shelters for people but with defending his actions against his critics. And that is really the more difficult phase of the work. Since Father has such a great heart it is the one which distresses him most. I think that he enjoys a good fight with the publicans and the crowd which wants to be free to purvey vice to the multitudes, but it hurts him to be forced to take a stand against other good, albeit misguided, Christians."

Eva's brow was creased in thought.

"Do you suppose, Bramwell, that we could arrange it so Father could take a journey around the world? He has always wanted to visit the places where the Salvation Army has been established. He wanted to do it with Mother. Could we plan it so that he would feel he was needed for such an assignment?" she asked.

"He is needed," Bramwell ejaculated fervently. "This is something that he should have done years ago. But how to arrange it!"

His brow furrowed.

"It should not be difficult," one of the staff officers said. "We could write a few letters to men who are strategically located in the United States, Australia, Canada, India and France, urging them to write the General to ascertain whether or not he could come out to visit them. Each one could speak about specific problems which only the General could solve."

"France and India would be easy," Eva said. "Catherine and Emma could take care of that."

"And George Railton has long wanted to have Father visit his stations in America," Bramwell added.

"But who will look after the work here?" one of the staff officers inquired.

"Haven't we all grown up in the Army?" Eva asked. "Some day the direction of the Army will fall on our shoulders. Father isn't going to be with us forever; but we'll have him much longer if we can take from his shoulders some of those problems which vex him so sorely."

"Eva's right," Bramwell added. "I can see the great change in him since Mother left us."

"Then let's do it at once," one of the officers remarked. "I'll write to Railton."

"It would probably be better if the letters went out from members of the staff instead of one of the Booths," Bramwell suggested. "Father would see through our strategy if either Eva or I wrote and if those who received our letters mentioned the fact that it was in reply to them that they were writing. Would you good people take care of the correspondence?"

144

"Of course," other officers chorused, "and we'll not mention your names."

One of them added, "And we'll write today."

They were as good as their word.

As a result of their correspondence George Railton wrote from the States, addressing the letter to the General,

> If you could only visit our stations in New York, Philadelphia, Chicago and San Francisco you could see for yourself what strides we have made. And it would give an enormous impetus to the work for our people to see you and share with you our successes and our problems. I did not say "failures" because we have had none of those. But our problems may either result in failures or successes. Won't you come and give us the incentive we need to sturdier efforts?

Tucker wrote from India,

> Selfishly we would love to have you visit us that we may see you again. Emma never confesses to homesickness but when her mother died she longed to be at home. Only the great distance which separates us kept her here. Now a visit from you, Sir, would inspirit her as nothing else could.
>
> But there are also enormous problems confronting us in the solution of which your counsel would prove invaluable. Our work so far has only been with the untouchables, but we must win the castes as well. Whether they will break down the caste system or not is problematic. It will probably take generations for that to be accomplished but if we can secure the co-operation and sympathy of the upper castes for our work we can win India. Then, too, the government is still maintaining a position of aloofness. Since I was a former government official it is especially difficult for me to approach the leaders. You could help us at this point.

"I must go overseas," the General announced after he had perused the many letters which arrived.

He was quite evidently unaware of the conspiracy which had prompted the missives.

"They held off writing me during Catherine's illness," he explained, "but now they insist that I must come. Do you think that you could take over our Darkest England project, Bramwell?"

"Not as well as you could, Father," Bramwell replied, "but I shall certainly do my best. And you have laid the groundwork for the entire program. If you will outline the next steps which you want us to take we shall try to go ahead with the program just as if you were here."

William's personal inclination had been to go to the United States first of all. The Army was still striving for the right to hold street meetings and parades in the leading cities of the country. In Buffalo, St. Louis, Sacramento and Colorado Springs the authorities opposed them. Several Salvationists were killed in San Francisco under what appeared to be exceedingly suspicious circumstances.

However, his desire to see his daughters who were serving overseas won out. Perhaps because he would not admit even to himself that family ties could possibly take precedence, he went first to Germany, with the intention of visiting France immediately thereafter and then going on to India.

But soon after he arrived in Hamburg he was homesick for London. "I am very down today," he wrote Bramwell, but added, "do stop sending out foolish instructions about my food."

The General discovered when he arrived on the continent that people were so eager to see and hear him that they would pay for the privilege. For this reason he rented large theaters and sold tickets to his lectures. And, quite possibly because they had to pay to hear him, the theaters and halls which were rented were always crowded to capacity. He expanded considerably on his "Darkest England" theme. Since he often took a walk at night he discovered that Hamburg and Frankfort were not different from London in the matter of unemployed vagrants. Other men — and even women and children — walked the streets as he did, but they had no lodgings to which they could go when they were worn out from their tramping.

And, while the Army had made brave beginnings in Germany, the Army citadels were makeshift. The General was disappointed in the quarters where the Salvationists met, forgetting that in England the Army had first met in a wool shop and a stable. He expected that he would find buildings in Germany for the corps comparable to those he had left in London.

But not even in London or Newcastle was he as royally feted as he was in Germany. He had dinner with Count Moltke and afterwards met with some of the leading capitalists of the country, challenging them to cope with the problems of unemployment and inadequate housing. At the suggestion of German friends he also decided to visit the Scandinavian countries. In Copenhagen throngs followed him on the streets as he strode along in his picturesque red and black uniform with its flowing cape. In a land of many beards his own bush adornment still stood out as exceptional.

He did not, however, have time to visit France as originally planned, due to word from England regarding obstacles which his Darkest England project was facing. Posthaste he returned to London.

His first conference upon his arrival was with his son.

"What's it all about, Bramwell?" he asked his son. "I thought you'd be able to handle everything in my absence."

"We could have done so, Father," he replied, "but committees are being set up to inquire into the affairs of the program, and the newspapers are attacking us, claiming that you have pocketed the money which has been raised and that you have used it for your own devices."

"Well, we have the perfect answer for that," the General replied. "Every penny which has been raised can be accounted for. What have you done to counter their claims?"

"Nothing so far. We felt that we should wait until you returned from overseas."

"Have you kept a file of the newspaper articles?"

"Yes. You can look them over if you want to. As a matter of fact we feel that many of the articles provide bases for libel suits."

"But we'll have no suits," the General retorted firmly. "The Salvation Army will never take such matters into court. We'll continue to answer our enemies and traducers by publishing the truth, but we'll never sue in a court of law to defend our integrity."

"But how else can we prove to the people of England that the charges against us are false?" Bramwell inquired. "Would it not be a good idea to bring suit and then, when the suit is won, return the amount of damages granted by the court to the people whom you had sued?"

"That would be possible, lad, but there is still a better way, and one which would also keep us out of court."

"But what other way. . . ."

"Secure the appointment of an impartial committee composed of some of the leading people of England to ask them to investigate our affairs."

"You're right as usual, Father," Bramwell replied ruefully, "but would anyone serve on that committee?"

"I think they would," William replied confidently.

Thereupon the General directed letters to a group of leading citizens. The letters read as follows:

Dear Friend:

During my recent absence from England, while I was making a tour of the European countries, visiting the various continental

147

posts of our Army, a series of charges was leveled at the Salvation Army and against me personally, alleging misuse of funds which had been raised for our "Darkest England" program.

We are desirous of submitting the aims of our entire program to an altogether unbiased committee. In order that the members of the committee shall be completely neutral we have chosen people who have no connection, so far as we know, with the Salvation Army or the "Darkest England" fund.

The entire list of people to whom I am addressing this request is as follows:

[Here the General gave the names of the people who were receiving these letters.]

I hope that you will agree to serve on this committee so that the people may know what are the facts regarding our "Darkest England" project.

I am, Sir, very respectfully yours,
William Booth,
General, Salvation Army.

The committee which the General had selected consisted of the following, all well known in politics or industry: Sir Henry James of Hereford, Chairman; Mr. Sydney Buxton, M. P.; Mr. Walter Long; Mr. Edwin Waterhouse, President of the Institute of Chartered Accountants; and Mr. C. Hobhouse, M. P., the Honorable Secretary. They were all men who were universally esteemed. No one could question their findings.

The committee waded through a mass of material, including letters which the newspapers and the headquarters staff of the Salvation Army had received, together with all of the account books of both the Salvation Army and the Darkest England fund. They then outlined their goal which, they indicated was that of finding answers for the three questions which they deemed most pertinent:

"1. Have the moneys which were collected by means of the appeal made to the public for 'In Darkest England and the Way Out' been devoted to the objects and expended in the methods set out in that appeal, and to and in no other?

"2. Have the methods employed in the expenditure of such moneys been, and are they, of a businesslike, economical, and prudent character, and have the accounts of such expenditures been kept in a proper and clear manner?

"3. Is the property, both real and personal, and are the moneys resulting from the above appeal now so vested that they cannot be applied to any purposes other than those set out in 'Darkest England,' and what safeguards exist to prevent the misapplication of such property and money, either now or after the death of Mr. Booth?"

The committee carefully examined all of the books of the Darkest England project as well as those of the Salvation Army. They criticized the Army for the manner in which the Deed of Trust had been drawn up, giving, as it did, almost unlimited power to the Commanding General, but noted that William Booth had in no wise abused the trust which had been confided to him.

The accounts were ascertained to be correct in every detail, and it was noted that General Booth, contrary to the charges which had been made against him, had received not so much as a single penny either from the Army or the Darkest England project. The summary of their findings noted that, "In examining the accounts, the Committee was careful to inquire whether any portion of the traveling expenses of the members of the Salvation Army had been borne by the Darkest England Fund, and whether Mr. Booth or any of his family have drawn any sums for their personal use therefrom. No such expenditure appears to have been incurred. There is no reason to think that Mr. Booth or any of his family derive, or ever have derived, benefit of any kind from any of the properties or money raised for the Darkest England scheme. Some members of the Booth family drew salaries from the spiritual wing of the Salvation Army and a list was put in from which it appears that Mr. Booth has received nothing from either side of the Salvation Army."

The committee added, "Mr. Booth has a small income partly settled on him by a personal friend and partly derived from the sale of his literary works, the amount and nature of which he explained to the Committee and which seems to them commensurate with the maintenance of his personal establishment."

The newspapers which had previously printed letters denouncing the Salvation Army and the Darkest England movement were glad to publish the report and some of the editors wrote special articles noting that the General's integrity had been proven beyond the shadow of a doubt. Whatever one might say of the methods and program of the Army, whether one agreed with them or not, at least it could not be charged that William Booth was using or had used the Army to advance his own fortunes.

"I think I'll be able to continue my interrupted journey around the world now," William remarked to Bramwell and other members of the headquarters staff. "And you needn't fear that we will be accused again of dishonesty, either you and the other officers of the Army, or the Booth family. Is there any reason that you can conceive why I can't set forth now?"

Bramwell shook his head.

"The storm's over, Father," he replied. "I think we should be able to carry on from this point."

"Then I can get out on the road again," the General announced.

And off he went but not immediately to foreign posts. The pain of the loss of Catherine was assuaged to a considerable extent by his preaching engagements in the many cities which he visited. And the old General attracted greater crowds than had attended the halls and theaters where he had held meetings in his youth. He intended to go overseas but he finally decided to stay in England, at least until the International Congress was convened in 1894. This was to be the jubilee year of his own conversion and he was exceedingly anxious to have a great conference.

No longer did he conceive of such an international meeting as a "War" Congress, which had been the title by which he had designated the first such meeting. On the present occasion, too, it would truly be an international gathering. Canada, the United States, India, the countries of Europe and even distant Java would be represented. Australia and New Zealand would have their delegations.

One of the principal topics for consideration at the International Congress would be the social work program of the Army. Many earnest Salvationists considered the Darkest England program no true part of the Army's work or, if they were willing to concede that it was a worthy program, believed that it could be better done by others. Recognizing the fact that the Darkest England program would be under attack at the Congress, the General decided to defend it first of all to his own people.

Therefore, in his initial speech, he lauded the program by saying that the social work of the Salvation Army was an expression of the religious conscience of mankind and was definitely *religious* work. Certainly the Lord would approve it or He would never have cited with such evident approbation the story of the good Samaritan. The General concluded a lengthy speech by insisting that religious work is the greatest of all social works. "You cannot make a man clean by washing his shirt. The Salvation Army will always be a great evangelizing organization. But it is now on the march towards redeeming the communities in which our people live."

He was greeted with a rousing ovation. If there were objectors they did not dare to voice their protests. Although to some extent against his own inclinations and desires, the Army was now committed to a program of social service. But the General had reluctantly conceded what the Army recognized, and that was that faith and works needed to go hand in hand.

CHAPTER 15

With the termination of the International Congress it was decided that the General should travel to the Far East to visit outstations of the Army.

"A Mediterranean tour would be good for him," Eva suggested to Bramwell. "I hope that he can see the sights along the way. Father and Mother always wanted to visit the Holy Land."

But when the subject was broached to him the General objected.

"I'll go through the Mediterranean on my way to India and Australia, of course," he agreed, "but I don't feel that I could stop in Nazareth or walk in the hills above Bethlehem without Mother."

"She will be with you every step of the way," Bramwell urged quietly.

"I realize that," the General acknowledged, "but it wouldn't be the same. I'm also confident that where she is now is the true Holy Land, for she is where our blessed Saviour resides. But I can't go to Palestine without her."

"Very well, Father," Bramwell said, "but if you change your mind . . ."

"I'll not," the General asserted positively.

He bought a ticket on a P. and O. liner which was to go through the Mediterranean but his destination would be Australia and New Zealand. The work had been opened in several of the cities of those far countries. The General had heard of the friendly way in which, according to the reports of his officers, the Army had been welcomed "down under." He was also eager to ascertain how England's experiment with an over-

151

seas colony of criminals had worked out. He felt that one of the countries where a modern colony of derelicts might be established would be one of the provinces of Australia. The other such location, he had decided, should be Canada. There was too much unrest in South Africa to make colonization there possible at the moment or for some time to come.

The General's dispatches, written en route, were for the most part undated and curt, but he gave exceedingly graphic word pictures of his experiences. A letter received from him in London, which was addressed to both Bramwell and Eva, gave the following impressions:

> Gibraltar . . . fabled Pillars of Hercules . . . monkeys sharing with Englishmen the defense of the Mediterranean for Queen. Make a note to see about establishing an outpost of the Army here.

He added as a postscript to his letter this note:

> Have now decided would like to stop at Palestine. Told you before that I didn't want to visit Holy Land without Mother, but wish now I had included it in my itinerary. However, our ship goes directly to Alexandria where this letter will be mailed, then through Red Sea. Moses pushed back waters there — or God did — to take *His* army through dry-shod.
>
> Aden . . . The Mail . . .
>
> I am living on potatoes, rice and fruit. Not much choice of the latter. But *plenty* and enough is as good as a feast. I am expecting an extra feed for dinner of macaroni and tomatoes.
>
> I don't think we ought to *fret* ourselves about *evil doers* — or about Officers and *others* who don't do quite as well as we think they ought to.
>
> I wish I was stronger! I don't think any of you have any idea of the amount of weakness and weariness, if not positive sickness, through which *I have to fight my way!* You see me under the stimulus of the *hour* or on the spur of the excitement caused by your intercourse — and are apt to infer wrongly as to my general condition. My life is *now a hard fight.*

Bramwell read the letter to Eva.

"Father is begging for sympathy again," he remarked. "I'll write him all the pertinent news but I'm certainly not going to be overly sympathetic with him."

"It has become second nature to him, Bram, to tell someone about his ills," Eva remarked. "Mother listened to him so patiently, you remember, and always felt so sorry for him."

"Well, I certainly can't take Mother's place," Bramwell objected.

"No. Of course not," Eva agreed. "But you will recall that even during her serious illness she would be greatly concerned for his health if he just had a slight cold."

"She was too good to him."

"Most wives are too good to their husbands," Eva rejoined tartly.

Bramwell laughed.

"You don't intend to be?"

"No."

"Well, then, dearest sister, you'll probably spend your life in blessed spinsterhood," Bramwell retorted.

"I shall be perfectly willing to continue in that state," Eva calmly replied. "In any event you know that a Booth is married to the Salvation Army, whether the Booth is male or female."

"That's true," Bramwell soberly agreed. "Well, it's settled then. I'll mail Father reports of the work. You write the intimate, personal letters if you wish to."

"I'll be glad to do that," Eva replied. "I know that the little details of our everyday life are what he really wants. He craves constant assurance of our love."

The General's next letter came from Aden. He had just received mail from home when he wrote. A ship had been wrecked in the typhoon and his observations, put down in his letter to Bramwell, were descriptive and productive of grist for the mill of his public addresses. Most of the General's potent preaching illustrations came from such contemporary sources. And every letter that he wrote had in it the elements of a sermon. His letter, laboriously written by hand noted:

> The *Paris* wrecked . . . on the rocks . . . Great efforts to save her. Many steamers tugged at her. Tons of rocks blasted. Given up.
> A Salvage Company appears.
> Now the world rings with the tidings. The *Paris* is floating. The beautiful ship is saved, towed into harbour, and with damages repaired is to resume her career.

Abruptly he added,

> This whole incident gave me an idea for a whopping sermon. See how it appeals to you. This is the outline in brief:
> The *Paris* impaled on a sharp projecting piece of Rock — she held together but any storm, etc. Rocks on it.
> Backslider.
> Tremendous efforts made to save her.
> No giving up.
> Never despair.
> Ingenuity succeeded.
> Yet it was all in the ordinary course of things.
> Tremendous satisfaction.

> More interest in *Paris* than in building new steamer.
>
> Left there, she was a constant reproach.
>
> Tremendous profit to the saviours. And she steams about, one of the best-known ships on the ocean.

Since Bramwell's wife had taken over the rescue homes for young women he added a suggestion for her:

> Why don't you suggest to her that she write a book on *How Our Girls Are Damned?* . . . Or, if she does not like swearing in her title, put it blasted, blighted, ruined, only it should be a good expletive.

His visit to India was exceedingly successful, but the General was welcomed in Australia as if he were a victorious warrior returning to his own country after a successful campaign. If his flamboyancy had been ridiculed in England it was regarded in Australia with respect. His host for the visit to the various political subdivisions of the country was Commissioner T. Henry Howard who had succeeded Ballington in command of the Australian forces.

The General preached with all of the fire he had shown in his youth, but there was a wistfulness in his messages which he had lacked earlier in his preaching career.

Howard warmly commended him and remarked on the interest with which the people listened to him.

"They're unlike any Englishmen I've ever known," the General commented.

Howard smiled.

"Don't use that word down here, General," he advised. "These people are not Englishmen and they resent being called English. They're Australians — and proud of it. Ballington spoke in one of our largest halls several years ago and he was almost hissed off the platform when he made that same mistake. But he recovered quickly and added, 'I meant Englishmen who had seen the light and emigrated to Australia.' They applauded him for that."

The General took advantage of this counsel that same evening.

"My dear friends," he said, "I was warned that I shouldn't speak of you as Englishmen — as if I ever would. No, you're not Englishmen although you sprang from that race of people. You're a rare new breed. As you are no doubt aware — my speech betrays me, I know — I *am* English. But I am altogether certain that if I had ever visited Australia in my youth I wouldn't have remained English for long. I would have been an Australian."

The General received the round of applause which he had anticipated and later told his wife about it.

"Catherine dearest," he said, looking at her picture, "we really had a crash tonight. They were ready to go down on their knees for the Lord. And I really think that this boy Howard makes a good commissioner — better, really, than Ballington. Ballington doesn't *stick*. He has the Booth impatience, and you know — better than anyone else — how impatient a Booth can be. But his impatience doesn't result in his doing something about a situation, which is Bramwell's method. No, indeed. His impatience results in his throwing up the sponge and going off to some other place or to some other movement. But say a good word to the Lord for Ballington. He's a good lad and the kind the Lord may — nay, will — find for him the place where he can be most useful for the Kingdom."

In the United States the General was received as enthusiastically as in Australia, but the people of America regarded him with even greater awe than did the Australians. Wherever he went he became an immediate center of attention, with pictures and stories concerning him in the newspapers, so that it became difficult for him to walk down any street without gathering a crowd about him. His cloak with its Salvation Army insignia embroidered on it, and his flowing beard, now sprinkled with white, immediately set him apart from others.

A ride in an open victoria down Market Street in San Francisco or State Street in Chicago became a triumphal procession, immediately attracting crowds.

"The whole thing is a crash," the General remarked aloud to Catherine as he went to the hotel one evening after speaking to a crowd which overflowed the auditorium. As Bramwell had predicted, the General's tour throughout the United States and Canada had a pronounced effect upon the two countries.

When it was completed William returned briefly to London to see his family and confer with the staff at International Headquarters.

After the conference was over Bramwell and Eva met in Bramwell's office.

"Father seems better than ever," Eva remarked.

"But notice how gray his hair has become — just since we last saw him," Bramwell replied. "And note the many new lines in his face."

"Yes, but he seems to be fully as alert as he has ever been," Eva remarked.

"He's buoyed up, that's certain, but I'm afraid that he was overworked on his voyage," Bramwell said. "And no sooner is he home than he wants to visit the Scandivanian countries. We should slow him down."

"No, no," Eva objected. "This has always been his life and never have his meetings been as fruitful as now. He is seeing the happy results of long, hard years of labor. Let him enjoy them while he can."

"I suppose you're right," Bramwell acknowledged, "but I'm afraid that Father may burn himself out. Even such an old warrior as he needs to take time out to regroup his forces for his next engagement. Frankly, when he goes off like this I fear that he may have a heart attack or a stroke."

"He may," agreed Eva, "but what if he does? This would be the way he would want to have death come — not in some old people's home where he would only vegetate."

Bramwell nodded his head in agreement.

"I imagine that you're right," he acknowledged.

So the General went to Copenhagen. His first report to Bramwell and Eva by letter was brief and succinct:

> Arrived safely Copenhagen at approximately 10:30 A.M.
> Press interviews at 11:00 A.M.
> Interview with the King and Queen in the afternoon.
> Most friendly. Interview lasted, to the amazement of the Equerry and the people in the anteroom, an hour and a quarter.
> The King expressed his interest in the Army and the pleasure with which he regarded our success.
> Was much impressed by the Queen. She appeared to be rather a serious personage. Dressed very neatly without any attempt to do the grand or queenly. Both expressed again and again their admiration of our work, and their sympathy with me.

Three days later Bramwell remarked to Eva, "Another letter from Father. This time he writes from Christiania. He is evidently enjoying himself thoroughly. Listen to this:

> Meeting in the Royal Opera House at 1:00 P.M. Fine audience — a real representation of the leading people of the city. Much liberty and great acceptance. Spoke an hour and three-quarters. At the close, the Vice-President of the Parliament rose spontaneously from his place, and gave expression to the thanks of the congregation for the Lecture, their admiration of our work, and their sympathy with the General.
> The entire audience rose to endorse the sentiment.

"Father is becoming a better correspondent," Eva remarked. "He actually completes some of his sentences."

Bramwell laughed heartily.

"I'm tremendously glad for him, but I never think of these engagements without realizing how much Mother would enjoy accompanying Father or, if she couldn't always be with him, at least receiving letters from him to tell her about the work," he remarked.

However, Bramwell's mother did hear from the General regularly.

Whenever a meeting was concluded and he would be giving it the usual after-meeting consideration he would say, always speaking aloud in the sanctuary of his hotel room or lodgings, "Well, Catherine, we really crashed through tonight."

To be sure, there were occasions when he would have to submit a negative report.

"I couldn't seem to get going tonight, dearest wife," he would say. "Some way or other I just failed to warm up."

But whenever the meeting was particularly successful and he would give her a glowing account of it he would add wistfully, "I hope that you were in the meeting. I miss you so, my Kate."

CHAPTER 16

In 1896 the prime minister of Great Britain, Mr. W. E. Gladstone, sent the General a personal invitation to visit him at Hawarden Castle. He apparently chose that location as one most calculated to allow for the freest exchange of thoughts between himself and his guest without interruption, instead of his office in London.

"This is a pleasure to which I have looked forward for a long time, Mr. Booth," Mr. Gladstone said. As an afterthought he added, "Or should I have addressed you as 'General'?"

The General's eyes twinkled.

"You may call me anything you want, Mr. Prime Minister," he replied. "I have been called many different things, some of the titles which have been applied to me being in no sense commendatory."

"I can well appreciate that," Mr. Gladstone said. "I, too, am apparently many different things to different people."

"I want you to know that I feel highly honored at the invitation to confer with you, Mr. Gladstone," the General said, "but I am somewhat curious to know the purpose of our conference. You don't ordinarily confer with evangelists, do you?"

Laughingly Mr. Gladstone replied, "Not ordinarily, no. But you are quite different from others of whom I have heard. You are the only evangelist I have ever known who is referred to as 'General.' How did you happen to obtain that rank?"

"I really didn't obtain it in any ordinary way," the General said. "You might say that I just appropriated it. Or perhaps I should say — since the idea didn't originate with me, that some of my co-workers decided that, since we were organized in a fashion similar to that of her Majesty's army, we should naturally assume army titles."

"And you became the General?"

"Yes, that was the rank accorded me."

"And how far does your authority extend?"

"To every place where we have commands."

"To your overseas organizations as well?"

"Yes."

"What do you call your immediate subordinates overseas?"

"Their rank is that of 'commissioner.' For instance, we have a commissioner in Canada, another in Australia, and one in India."

"Are these all Englishmen?"

"Chiefly so," the General replied, "although, when the Army is established in the future, they will probably be nationals."

"Do you still find opposition to the Army in various parts of the world?"

"Yes, we do. And in some places the opposition is particularly violent."

"Much of it, I suppose, from Roman Catholics?"

"No, that's not true. We have been opposed by clergymen of many different communions, but no greater opposition from Catholic priests than from Protestant ministers — and some priests and ministers are warm friends of the Army. It may interest you to know that among our officers are some who are Roman Catholic, and Cardinal Manning, the leading prelate of our own country, has been most sympathetic to the Army and its objectives."

"I am indeed surprised to hear of the opposition of the Protestant clergy overseas," Mr. Gladstone remarked.

"But we expected it, Mr. Prime Minister," William countered. "Many clergymen in England stood against us when the Army was first organized here."

158

Mr. Gladstone changed the subject.

"Now to a different topic," he said. "Naturally, considering the influence which the Army exerts today, and having in mind the tremendous number of people whom you have enrolled, I am interested in the choice of your successor — just as the Crown is interested in knowing who are the potential future prime ministers of the realm. What provision has been made for the election of the one who will replace you?"

"He has already been chosen," the General replied. "His name is revealed in a document which has been placed in a sealed envelope and is in the custody of the Army Solicitors. That envelope will be opened when I die, and the one whom I have chosen will be my successor."

With a sly smile Mr. Gladstone inquired, "General, are you a Protestant?"

"Assuredly," the General replied, "although, as I have told you, I have many warm friends who are Roman Catholic priests. They have been most sympathetic towards the work of the Army."

"Including Cardinal Manning, as you said?"

"Yes, including the Cardinal."

"He is not only a great churchman," Gladstone remarked fervently, "but a true Englishman as well."

"He surely is."

"The reason I have inquired, however, is because I detect evidences of what I would call Roman Catholic techniques in your program," Mr. Gladstone continued.

"Catholic techniques!" exclaimed the General incredulously. "What do you mean?"

"Perhaps I shouldn't call them techniques or methods. Instead, I should have remarked that in some respects you outdo the Catholics. For instance, the reigning pope never has the opportunity to appoint his successor although you do. Yet, since it is assumed that he is in direct descent from Saint Peter, it would seem as if some such method as you employ would have become the way of assuring the continuity of the Church. Yet the incumbent pontiff has nothing to do with the selection of the one who will succeed him. That is left in the hands of the cardinals who assemble shortly after his death."

"Yes, that's true," the General agreed.

"Then perhaps you will acknowledge that the Salvation Army is much more hierarchical than the Roman Church," Mr. Gladstone remarked with a sly smile.

"No, I don't," William replied. "The Army is not the Church. It is not a branch of the Church. The Army is the Army and, please God, that is what it will always remain."

"But you hold services in much the same fashion as a church does," objected Gladstone.

"Yes," agreed William, "and the House of Commons and the American Senate open their deliberations with prayer: yet you would never call either a church."

"God forbid!" remarked Mr. Gladstone, laughing.

At this point Mrs. Gladstone interrupted.

"Can you break off your interesting conversation for a spot of tea?" she inquired.

"Gladly, my dear," Mr. Gladstone replied. "We have really reached the end of our meeting and, let me say, my lady, that it has been most interesting and informative. It was kind of you to drop in to see me, General."

"I am most indebted to you, sir, for your goodness in welcoming me to your home. Nor shall I take advantage of your hospitality. I realize that one who is in such a situation as yours must not commend such a movement as ours or you would be constantly importuned to endorse other organizations," William remarked.

"William is constantly asked to do just that," Mrs. Gladstone interjected. "However, since I'm not in politics I can express myself freely, and I must say that I am heartily in favor of your movement, and I pray for its success nightly. Nor do you need to hesitate to use my name if it will be of value to you."

The General's eyes twinkled.

"Since you and the prime minister are one so far as the Empire is concerned — just as Mrs. Booth was as vital a part of the Army as I ever was — I shall still not presume upon your kind hospitality by even suggesting that you endorse our program," he said.

The prime minister laughed.

"You can be assured, nevertheless, where the Gladstones stand, General," he said, "and you can be certain that you have our earnest prayers for the welfare of your fine organization."

After the General had taken his leave of the Gladstones he reported to Bramwell that "among the many things carefully considered and experimentally known to W. E. Gladstone are the governing influences of the Holy Spirit and the saving grace of God."

Although the General was true to his promise and he refused to make capital of the interview with the prime minister — or possibly because he failed to do so — many of the leaders in the empire sought him out.

Among such leaders were Lord Loch and the South African empire builder, Cecil Rhodes.

When the General had a note from Mr. Rhodes, asking him if he would allow the latter to visit the farm colony at Hadleigh he remarked to Bramwell, "He is a man of destiny and power. He can either plunge our country into war or make an end to dangerous tension by reasonable and conciliatory diplomacy. Few men of our generation possess as much power for good or evil as he does."

"But you are one of those men, Father," Bramwell remarked quietly.

"I have no such power, son, and you know it," the General replied testily.

"You have more power than you realize," Bramwell asserted.

Shortly afterwards, in May, 1898, the General took Lord Loch and Cecil Rhodes to the farm colony, traveling by rail.

Rhodes was tremendously interested in what he saw, and with his shrewd eyes observed everything, the neat rows of vegetables, the well-kept houses for the workers, the gleaming dining room, the men busy with multitudinous tasks.

"You said, I think, that these men have been drunkards?" Rhodes asked the General.

"Many of them — probably the majority — have been," the General replied, "and the magistrates before whom they appeared have evidently regarded them as incurable."

"But they all look fit — as if they haven't been on a drinking bout for months," Cecil Rhodes continued.

"They haven't."

"Well, you have assuredly wrought a miracle in their lives then," the South African millionaire observed.

"No, sir. You're wrong. We haven't," William objected. "If a miracle has been wrought it has been accomplished by God. And, quite frankly, we have been more concerned about the souls of these men than about their bodies. All we have done has been to remove temptation from their path. God has done the rest."

"Well, judging from external signs I would say that the men have certainly benefited by their life at the farm."

"Bodies that are fit reflect souls that are in tune with God."

Their conversation continued in the railroad coach, Rhodes

still marveling over the changes which had been wrought in the men who had gone to the Salvation Army farm.

Finally, as they sat side by side in the coach, the General placed his hand on Rhodes' knee.

"What about your own soul, Mr. Rhodes?" he inquired. "What about yourself? You are a man upon whom much now depends for the welfare of mankind. Tell me, how is it with your soul?"

Lord Loch lifted his eyebrows in surprise. In his circles men didn't mention the human soul. Was the General intent on conducting an evangelistic meeting in a railroad carriage?

Rhodes paused for a moment before he made reply. Then he remarked quietly, "Well, General, I must admit that it's not quite so well with my soul as I could wish."

"Do you pray?" asked the General.

"Sometimes," Cecil Rhodes replied, "— but not quite so often as I should."

"Would you be willing to have me pray with you now?" the General inquired.

Lord Loch was embarrassed. He turned his face away, fixing his glance on a distant brook fringed with willows.

But Cecil Rhodes' eyes brightened. He looked eagerly at the General and wistfully made reply, "I'd appreciate it greatly if you would, sir."

The two men slipped from their seats, down onto their knees, and the General prayed for the soul of the South African colossus. He prayed that Rhodes might be guided by the power of the Holy Spirit in making decisions which might affect the destinies of many of the nations of the world. Then he added simply, "And, Lord, if it is Thy will, save the soul of this man. Show him that only as he dedicates himself to Thy cause and kingdom can he be of service to this country and to the world."

Then he added, "And may Thy holy will be done, and make this, Thy servant, voluntarily and happily obedient to Thy will. In the name of Him who gave Himself into Thy hands, even Thy Son, Jesus Christ, our Lord. Amen."

"Amen," echoed Cecil Rhodes fervently.

Immediately afterwards Rhodes took the General's hand.

"I hope that you will continue to pray for me," he said, "for I shall need your prayers."

"You can be assured that I will," the General promised him. Back at his lodgings in London the General shared the experience with Catherine, speaking to her as if she were still present with him.

"It will be a great victory for the Kingdom, Kate, if Mr. Rhodes comes through. You can tell the Father and our Lord Jesus Christ that. Mr. Rhodes is almost to the point of decision now, I believe, but I don't think he has ever really crashed through the barrier," he said aloud. "But we'll pray for the man and you know what great things can be wrought by prayer.

"But why am I saying these things to you? You know the secrets of the universe now. You have *seen* Jesus. You've met our Father face to face. I can't tell you anything — but I'm still going to talk with you about all the important decisions which I must make."

That same fall he discussed with Bramwell the idea of taking another journey around the world in order to visit all of the Salvation Army posts, should that be possible.

"I probably couldn't visit them all in a lifetime. And when I had finished such a journey I'd have to start over again to visit the new posts which would have sprung up while I was on my way. But if I can just visit the countries in which we have work that would be sufficient. But, son, I do wish that Mother had lived so that she could have gone with me."

"She'll be with you, Father. Never fear," Bramwell assured him. "And I'm all for this voyage. You started out once before, you will recall, and then had to come back here because of Mother's health. Now, by all means, you ought to go."

"I shall," the General announced decisively, "and I'm aware, son, of the fact that you and the staff are perfectly capable of handling the Army's affairs. You've demonstrated your abilities perfectly well these several years past. I'm really an anachronism now. I just get in the way of you fellers who do all the work."

Bramwell smiled.

"We know you won't live forever, General," he said. "We don't expect you to but when you finally join Mother you will leave a great void. You're the most precious asset that the Army has today. To many of our people — and to me also — you *are* the Army. William Booth and the Salvation Army are synonymous terms."

The General's eyes misted.

"Whether that's true or not it's good of you to say so, son," he said.

"It's true," Bramwell assured him.

"Well, if I make this trip. . . ."

"You must."

"Don't interrupt," the General objected with a flash of his old fire. "I was just going to say that when I go I'll plan to keep you informed of what happens along the way."

"Wonderful!" Bramwell exclaimed. "We'll have a special column in 'The War Cry' for your observations."

That evening the General told Catherine all about the proposed journey and concluded his recital of the plans by adding, "He's a good boy, Kate, a good boy, and a credit to you. And he looks more like you every day. Thank goodness he doesn't have the long Booth nose which the Lord gave to me."

CHAPTER 17

With the turn of the century the General was on tour, part of the time in England, and part of the time in some remote corner of the globe. Wherever he went he faithfully reported the events of his travels to his children.

Bramwell, as chief of staff, was faced with the major decisions of Army policy, where to establish a new post, upon whom they might call to secure a contribution for a new men's hostel, who should be the Salvationist in charge of an area and what his or her rank should be.

"Father evidently kept all these things in his head," he remarked to Eva. "We must get everything down in record books instead. And we must give more responsibility to area commanders, and train them to give similar responsibility to those who serve in their commands. Decisions shouldn't be made here in London which affect Hongkong, Madras, Amsterdam, Frankfort or Chicago. And the Army shouldn't be a private concern of one family, the Booths. It is much bigger than that family."

"True," Eva replied, "but as you have noted so often, as long as Father lives the Salvation Army and William Booth will be synonymous. Look at the headlines in the American papers: 'General William Booth Receives Keys of City'; 'Booth Speaks at City Auditorium to Overflow Crowds.' By comparison it's hard to imagine the times past when here in England Father would have to debate whether or not he would be justified in renting a vacant store building for three months."

164

"I'm glad that this is happening," Bramwell said. "Father is finally reaping the rewards of the struggles of his youth. But when he passes from the scene the Army must be so strong that it will not need to depend upon him — or one of us. And it's up to the two of us to see that that happens."

While Bramwell and the staff struggled in London, however, the General went on with his tour. Norway, Sweden, Russia, China — he visited them all. Offerings for his work were so large that Bramwell appointed a secretary to go along with him.

"Father would travel third class if he could and eat his meals in some little out-of-the-way restaurant in order to put all of the money back into the work. We'll see that the secretary takes care of that. "For the first time in his life Father can have a few of the creature comforts," Bramwell told the staff.

One change was made in their original plans. Irish Peter, who had served as the General's bodyguard years before, would go along to take care of travel details, the purchase of tickets, the hiring of cabs, all the matters which would be vexing at times and were always time-consuming. He was not needed any longer to protect the General. He was no longer menaced.

Captain Henry Kitching would serve as the secretary to handle the General's correspondence and keep the accounts. He was a young Salvationist who had previously been a clerk in a barrister's office.

"But I'll keep my own diary," William protested when he was told of these arrangements.

"Of course, Father," Eva said placatingly. "But we felt that Irish Peter and Henry would make it easier for you to get about. You need someone just for company in your travels."

"I have someone who is always with me," the General said.

"Whom do you mean?" Eva asked.

"Your mother, of course," the General said. "She is always with me."

"Yes, to be sure," Eva replied, tears misting her eyes.

The General, therefore, set in motion plans to go still farther afield and to spend a longer time abroad than he had on any previous voyage. But with the relief of Mafeking and the final termination of the Boer War the General decided that he should make plans to establish an overseas colony somewhere in South Africa. So again he postponed a visit overseas. London was the place where the funds for the colony would have to be raised.

Rhodesia seemed to be the best available site for the colony. It was far enough from the source of the heaviest fighting to have escaped the aftermath of war and the climate was such that his people would not have to adjust themselves to tropical conditions.

Hence he found himself tied down in England with numerous conferences. Coupled with the need for such meetings was the fact that there had been financial difficulties which came as an outgrowth of the American depression of 1903. The General felt that his presence was required in England to make day by day decisions for the Army.

So many people of note had become interested in the overseas colonies that he decided it would be wise to capitalize on their interest. One outstanding noble, Lord Rosebury, had committed himself to the program and offered his assistance in dealing with the government.

The General's diary for the period indicated something of the awe which he felt at being admitted to the presence of members of the House of Lords and Commons and, either for his own sake or for Catherine's, he engaged in the pleasant practice of name-dropping as he made his daily entry in his diary. It is also possible that he wrote with an awareness of the fact that at some future date his diary would be published.

The General had reached the decision that his overseas project merited financial support from the government, and he did not hesitate to request it. This was actually the first time in his life that he had come to feel that any project with which he was associated should have subsidies of any kind from the government of His Majesty. It represented a radical change in his way of thinking, for his manner of life up to this point had been exceedingly independent.

His approach to Lloyd George who, at that time, was serving as Chancellor of the Exchequer, was blunt and to the point.

Having been ushered into the Chancellor's presence the General said boldly, "I want one hundred thousand pounds for our colony of workless people which will be established in Africa. This sum will be conditional upon the South African Company's providing one hundred fifty thousand pounds — in conjunction with other companies or groups."

"You think that you can get that much from Rhodes?" Lloyd George bluntly inquired.

"I believe that he is interested," the General cannily asserted.

"Can we be assured that the colony will be successful?" Lloyd George countered.

"No. It will only be experimental in its early stages. We have no assurance that unemployed people who have grown up in damp, chilly, foggy London will be happy on the African veldt. We can only hope that they will be. And we can't even be assured that they will stay out there once they are settled," the General replied.

Lloyd George nodded his bushy head.

"I appreciate your frankness, General," he said. "You don't make rosy promises which are impossible of fulfillment. And you seem to have your feet on the ground."

"Mr. Chancellor, I grew up in the hard school of experience," the General replied with a smile. "I believe that, once a man is saved by grace, he will try to live a more useful life; but I also know that sometimes the poor chap may stumble and fall. I know that he is worth saving and, once he has been saved, worth keeping in a situation where he can continue in fellowship with God."

"You indicated that you wanted one hundred thousand pounds. Do you want all that money at once?"

"No," the General replied. "I'd like to have twenty thousand pounds per annum for the next five years. That investment should give us time to prove whether or not the plan is feasible."

Lloyd George introduced the General to Winston Churchill. They met quite by accident in a corridor of the House. Churchill had served as a correspondent in the Boer War and was beginning his meteoric career in politics, serving at the time as President of the Board of Trade.

Churchill had already acquired a reputation for skepticism regarding the clergy. Although he was essentially a deeply religious man he had little regard for bishops and popular ministers since he suspected them of insincerity. But he met his match in the General of the Salvation Army — and was delighted with the General's bluntness which was so much like his own.

When Lloyd George introduced them the General set Mr. Churchill back on his heels by remarking caustically, "Oh, I don't want to meet Mr. Churchill except in a room with seconds and a brace of pistols."

Young Churchill was somewhat taken aback by the General's blunt statement which was so similar to one which he himself might have uttered.

"Come," he demanded, "what have I done?"

"Kept me waiting and expecting for many long months, and then dismissed me with a curt statement," the General retorted.

He referred to correspondence with Churchill regarding the Darkest England project.

"Indeed!" Churchill replied, "I did all that I could to bring the matter off. I'm sorry I couldn't put it over for you."

The General gave him a piercing glance and nodded his head.

"Well, Sir, I believe you did," he agreed.

Mr. Churchill extended his hand.

"Come to my office sometime so that we can have a private conference," Mr. Churchill said as they shook hands.

"I'll be glad to," the General assured him.

For the next several years the General bent all of his energies to the development of his colonies plan. He was in and out of the Houses of Parliament constantly, conferring with one government official after another.

Among the many conferees were Herbert Asquith and Arthur Balfour, both, like Lloyd George, destined to be prime ministers, and many other notables. They were much interested in the General's plan but were greatly concerned with other plans for the alleviation of poverty. Asquith advocated unemployment insurance and sought to increase job opportunities. The General had come to believe wholeheartedly that his Darkest England program was the basic design for curing the twin ills of unemployment and poverty. They considered it an excellent plan but only one of many.

"Father is so completely enamored of his scheme that he can't see any other," Bramwell remarked to Eva.

"Of course," she replied. "That's Father's way. If he hadn't believed years ago that the Salvation Army was the greatest force for evangelism in the world there wouldn't have been any Army."

"But he was younger then," Bramwell remarked.

"Yes, younger and stronger. And his age counts against him when he's dealing with younger men," Eva said.

"I wish we could get him to slow down."

"You'll never be able to do so."

"No, I don't suppose so. Not until he breaks down will we be able to bring a halt to his activity."

The General went on with his work. He had become so concerned about the Darkest England program that he wanted to go to Rhodesia to see for himself what land might be available for colonization. But while he was there he decided that he would also like to see the other colonies in South Africa and especially visit the cities of Johannesburg and Bloemfontein.

Lord Rosebury suggested that someone else make the voyage.

"At your age don't you believe it's too risky? You're seventy-nine now — not twenty-nine," Rosebury reminded him.

"I never consider risks when my duty calls me," the General retorted.

"But does duty call you, or are you just trying to prove to yourself that you can do it?" Rosebury objected.

"I don't consider age an obstacle — and I'm not trying to prove anything. If my age has anything to do with it I merely want to see the foundations of the colony laid while the Lord still spares me."

So William started out. Peter Monk accompanied him to look after his comfort so far as possible, but Peter was almost the General's age. Henry Kitching was also with him but he couldn't slow down the impetuous General.

Soon the latter was meeting with the political leaders of the various colonies. Evenings he would note down his activities in his diary:

"Lunched with the Governor of Cape Colony, Sir Walter Hely-Hutchinson.

"On returning to the Hotel I found a card from the Prime Minister, Mr. Merriman. He is residing at the Hotel and wished an interview. I looked in on him and Mrs. Merriman at 6:25.

"He is a forceful and capable man. Very tall. He must be six feet five inches at least. He threw plenty of cold water on the Rhodesian Scheme, and I put all the religion into him I could. They say he is an infidel. I don't know; he was very civil, nay, kindly, with me — but full of unbelief about any good coming out of my colonization plans. Oh, oh, oh, who can decide when so many professed experts disagree?"

At Johannesburg the General's host was Mr. Abe Bailey and he noted down faithfully the details of their conferences.

"After lunch I had a long talk with him respecting Rhodesian affairs. I found him deeply interested and under the supposition that everything was settled, and that I was to inaugurate the Scheme. He was vexed to find that the things were still in the air. . . .

"Since he owns the most important newspapers in the country he is going to wire the government tomorrow morning to tell them that if they will push the Scheme he will help them. He reckons that he has great influence with them. I imagine that he does."

At Bloemfontein he nightly made notations:

"The Governor, Sir Hamilton Goold-Adams, is a remarkably agreeable person. Has resided many years in Africa — was General in Command in Rhodesia during the Matabele rebellion and was Governor of the Orange Free State during the Boer War.

"He is much interested in my colonization plans, presided at my evening lecture, and, generally speaking, made my stay agreeable."

For some time the General had been troubled by what seemed to be failing sight. His African visit apparently aggravated that condition and he mentioned it to Captain Kitching.

"It baffles me, boy," he said. "I can't seem to read the newspapers and magazines any more. However, I suspect that the ailment is a common one. Old age is just catching up with me."

"Nonsense, Sir," Henry Kitching protested. "You've just been straining your eyes too much. But I do think it might be wise to return to England. You could go to one of those eye specialists and have him examine you. Haven't you accomplished all you set out to do?"

"We haven't completed our preparations for the project yet."

"Won't everything depend upon the attitude of the Home Office, however? If the Home Secretary is agreeable, haven't you reached the point now where you could actually begin to send men out here?"

"Undoubtedly."

"Well, then, why not return to England?"

The General turned to Peter Monk.

"What think you, my sage friend?" he inquired.

"The capting is advisin' you well," Peter replied. "Better do as he says."

"Then heigh-ho for England," William replied with seeming light-heartedness.

When the General returned to England Bramwell made arrangements for him to be examined by Dr. Bell-Taylor, a famous ophthalmologist of Nottingham. By the time he appeared

for examination it had become almost impossible for the General to read.

Dr. Taylor examined the General's eyes and reported cataracts on both of them. One had reached the point where an operation would be feasible; but Dr. Taylor counseled waiting for the other cataract to ripen, suggesting that if he would do so both could be removed at once.

The General returned to London for a short waiting period, and apparently immediately forgot about his cataracts as he considered critical news concerning the Rhodesian colony program. It seemed to be hopelessly bogged down in politics. Everyone was in favor of the project but it became enmeshed in yards and yards of red tape.

But now another project engaged the General's attention and he threw himself heartily into it. He began to feel that the greatest need of the Army was a training school for staff officers. His visits with Salvationists overseas convinced him that many of them were so inadequately prepared for their work that they missed entirely the purposes and aims of the Army.

He had previously decided that the publication of a book of Army regulations would be sufficient for all the officers but now he was convinced that a training program was also necessary.

"It would be wonderful if Father could give the last years of his life to this work," Bramwell remarked to Captain Kitching. "There is no one who can so inspirit men and women to give themselves heart and soul in the Lord's service as he — and no one has made the sacrifices necessary to be a good officer as he has."

"But you couldn't confine his activity to the school," the captain replied.

Bramwell gave a wry grin.

"As well try to chain the lightning," he admitted.

Thus, up to the very moment that he went into the hospital for his operation, the General was busy, making plans for his training center, laying other plans for additional phases of the Army's work.

On December 16, 1908, he had his first operation which was performed at Guy's Hospital in London. He outlined the course of the day's activities in his diary. The first portion was written early in the morning before he was prepared for surgery, the remaining portion the following day. This was his entry:

"This is the day fixed for the operation. It is to be performed by Mr. Higgins, chief oculist on the hospital staff. I

hope the Lord will hold and guide his hands, and make this thing a success.

"Just got a letter from some friend at Bournemouth who says that he had five operations on his eyes, and that they were all a failure, and he had arranged to have his eyeball taken out on the Saturday, but on the day previous it took a turn for the better, and finally his sight came back and he has seen all right for the last four years. He attributes this restoration to the prayers of the Salvationists round and about.

"Twelve Noon. The nurse, about whom we felt a little curious, has just arrived. She seems a kind person — friendly and manageable. I don't get on well with hard, dictatorial members of this class.

"Shortly after, I was summoned upstairs with the announcement that the doctors had arrived, and that all was ready. I found the doctor with his shirt sleeves turned up, looking like business, and I was requested to sit down, and receive what I suppose was a baptism of cocaine in both eyes, and then undressed, got myself ready for bed, after which I mounted the operating table that had been extemporized in the middle of the room.

"It was three o'clock. The afternoon was foggy — the light consequently imperfect, but the doctor announced that he had brought with him an electric lamp which would enable him to operate without the light of day.

"I must say I felt rather curious as I laid myself down, and as he grasped my hand and commenced his work, but I simply felt that all I could do was, as I said to the operator when he was giving me some directions — 'All right, I am in the hands of God and you.'

"The effect of the cocaine was marvelous. After putting his needle into the eye in order to make a stitch to hold it in position, he thrust his knife into it — turned it round and then the darkened lens was brought forth. A little friction of the eyelid on the eyeball, very gently done, finished the operation. The actual work on the eye did not last more than two minutes. Both eyes were then bandaged up with sticking-plaster to prevent any movement whatever; a pad of wadding held in its place, elastic bands round the head completed the business, and I was piloted to bed, and lay down, full of gratitude that the long-looked-for was successfully commenced. I have to spend 48 hours in this entire darkness before the doctor is to remove the bandage to inspect his work."

172

On the twenty-first day of December he dictated an entry for his diary which his secretary set down in the book:

"Received a kind message of sympathy from Her Majesty, the Queen, reading as follows: 'Have felt so much for you, and hope the operation successful, and trust you are getting on towards complete recovery, and that the sight you need so much will soon be completely restored.   THE QUEEN.'"

When Captain Kitching read the message to him there flashed in his mind the word which he wanted Catherine to receive, "We should have dropped in on Her Majesty the day that we had our picnic in the park, dear. Maybe Her Majesty would have been glad to see us after all."

But aloud he dictated the reply to her telegram:

"General Booth thanks Her Majesty for Her gracious sympathy with him in the operation he has found necessary, and for the kind expressions in her telegram. Mr. Higgins has just seen the eye and says that it could not possibly be doing better. The General begs to offer his best wishes for Her Majesty's happiness."

CHAPTER 18

Early in 1909 the General was back at work again, keenly interested in all phases of the movement as before, and with his sight restored. In February he paid another visit to the Scandinavian countries where crowds greeted him. Concluding a successful preaching mission in Stockholm he decided that the time was ripe to visit Russia.

Yet every effort that he put forth to secure permission to visit either Russia or Finland was thwarted. The Swedes had told him so much about the Finns that it was the one country in the world which he especially wanted to visit. But the prohibition was final. General Booth was not wanted in either country.

However, whenever obstacles were placed in the General's way he always accepted the battle. Since he was forbidden access to either Finland or Russia they became the countries which it was incumbent upon him to visit. Brushed off by the Russian ambassador, he called upon the British representative in Stockholm.

"We're not at war with Russia, are we?" he inquired of the ambassador.

"We're usually on the verge of it," the ambassador replied.

"I presume we are, but if we are not actually engaged in hostilities, by what right do they refuse access to their country to a subject of His Majesty?" the General demanded.

"Oh, any nation may decide whether or not it is willing to admit citizens of another," the ambassador explained.

"A high-handed insult to His Majesty!" the General thundered.

"No, I wouldn't so describe it," the ambassador replied mildly. "Rather, I should say the Russians are not in favor of permitting a foreign general of an army to cross their boundaries or those of Finland."

"But the Salvation Army stands for peace and good will, the love of God. . . ."

"Quite," the ambassador agreed urbanely.

But the General had not finished. His determination to penetrate the borders of the two countries, with Finland in subjection to Russia, endeared him to the redoubtable Swedes who admired that kind of stubbornness. Both King Gustav and Prince Bernadotte, his brother, had become warm friends of the General, and Sweden had become an outpost of the Army.

The Lutheran Church, the state church of Sweden, sensed that the Salvation Army was not a potential ecclesiastical rival but was, instead, an ally. The Archbishop of Upsala, titular head of the church, not only gave personal endorsement to the Army and its General but gladly appeared on the platform with General Booth to give evidence of his interest in the work of the Army.

Because of intervention on the part of the king and Bernadotte the way suddenly opened for the General to visit St. Petersburg. The prohibition against his preaching was not relaxed but when he arrived in the city which was then the capital of the Russian empire he had numerous conferences with royalty and with leading noblemen.

"I suspect that they are fully as much in need of Salvation as the humblest peasant in this cold land," he noted in a letter to Eva, "and all of them seem to be afraid to permit me to preach to the serfs. I feel as Paul did when he was a prisoner in Rome. He had friends in the emperor's palace who were eager to listen to him but he was still in bonds. Unlike Paul, I'm not permitted to converse with the common people."

Although he had made these many friends in Russia he could not open the door for the Army to enter. Discouraged, therefore, he returned to England. By this time he was treated much like an elder statesman of the Empire. Queen Victoria was dead and Edward VII who had long been the General's friend was on the throne. The doors of Buckingham Palace were always open to him but he conferred more often with Queen Alexandra than with the king. He even enlisted the queen's services in an attempt to secure permission to return to Russia to establish the Army there.

She arranged for a conference with the empress dowager of Russia but it was to no avail. The dowager queen was frank in explaining the reasons for the Russian ban on preaching.

"The state church will never agree to the establishment of such an organization as yours," she said. "The czar would have no objection to it but our metropolitans regard the Salvation Army as another church. . . ."

"Which it is not," the General replied flatly, daring to interrupt royalty when his beloved Army was under fire.

"Which you assert is not a church," the empress agreed, adding, "yet which they believe is such."

Since the dowager empress apparently could do little to help him the General abandoned the idea, at least for the time being, of establishing the Army in Russia. Calls for his services in various parts of England had piled up to such an extent that he felt he should start on another tour across country. Possibly the various posts sensed that he would not be available much longer. As a result he was given a reception wherever he went which made the tour a triumphal procession.

One of the most touching experiences on the journey occurred at Hereford where he was the guest of Bishop Perceval, a man of approximately the same age as the General. One of the aides who accompanied him on the journey wrote Bramwell about the occurrence:

> The General has been having more and more trouble with his eye and also seems to feel that his span of life is nearing its end, and he has found in his Lordship a kindred soul. I had prepared his room for the night and went into the bishop's study to suggest to the General that he retire for the night.
>
> I found the two old veterans down on their knees praying.
>
> I shall never forget the earnestness depicted on both their faces as they pleaded with God for the Salvation of the people, and for His blessing on their respective labors.
>
> I stood with bowed head, fearing lest I should disturb them by leaving the apartment.

Presently the General lifted his head, and looking into the Bishop's face with an intensity of purpose, said, "My Lord, give me your benediction." Immediately the Bishop placed his hand upon the head of our beloved General and gave him the blessing. "And now," said his Lordship, "give me your blessing, General," and in response the General placed his hand upon the Bishop's head and called down upon him the blessings of Almighty God.

I do not think that I shall ever forget the sacred solemnity of that moment.

The next week the General entered a nursing home in London for an operation on his right eye. On August 21 the operation was performed for the removal of a cataract. Unfortunately the operation resulted in his becoming blind in this eye although he retained the sight of his left orb.

His children visited him in the nursing home and usually found him exceedingly cheerful. But one day he opened his heart to Eva.

"I sincerely hope that before long I can join your dear mother," he said. "We have been separated for much too long a time. And yet I have the feeling that I must stay on here. There is still so much to do. And there has never been such a time for the preaching of Salvation as today."

"We hope you'll stay, General," Eva replied quietly. "The Army needs you and, never forget, Mother is always close by your side."

"Aye, that she is," he asserted confidently, "and I suppose that she can wait."

Since the General's recovery was rapid his departure from life, which he deemed imminent, was indefinitely postponed. Yet the General felt more than ever Catherine's nearness. She seemed to be working with him in all that he undertook. At the same time it was noted that the older he became the more tolerant he was.

His theological position did not change. Hellfire and brimstone still entered into his preaching. But the General's attitude toward sinners did change; and he came to believe more and more that it was his mission not only to save people from eternal hellfire but to rescue them from a hell on earth.

It was still a basic tenet of his faith that a willful sinner was forever on the side of everlasting evil, and that he would receive the just deserts of his evil ways in a literal hell, but Salvation had a new meaning for him, particularly as it related to little children. He wanted to save them from poverty, from bare existence in foul slums.

Eva reported that when they were visiting in Chicago she had persuaded him to lie down one afternoon. He had met at luncheon some of the leading businessmen and had earnestly asked for their cooperation in providing decent homes for the poor people of the metropolis.

"Now you won't move, will you, darling?" she asked her father.

"Not a step," he promised.

But a few minutes later, from the adjoining room which she occupied, she heard him moving around. She opened the door and found him pacing up and down.

"Father!" she exclaimed. "You promised faithfully that you would lie still."

"Oh, I know, I know," he retorted impatiently, "but I've been thinking of the way little children suffer, the children in the large cities, and I can't rest. I can't rest."

On April 10 he wrote in his diary:

"I am eighty-one today. Reckoned on a quiet Sabbath with time for profitable reflections, but alas! how differently it has turned out. I suppose it has been one of the most harassing days I have experienced for some time. My head was swimming, off and on, from morning to night; but swimming or not, I was persuaded into doing some seven more messages [birthday reflections for the various papers], finishing up with the Times at nearly 10:00 on my bed worn out.

"Some things may be said against the course pursued, but I endeavored to put into every message some real Salvation Army doctrine, and to urge the responsibility resting on everyone for his own Salvation and the Salvation of his neighbors. If there is anything in preaching, surely the words I sent, which must have passed before the eyes of millions of people, must do some good. Anyway, they are intended to do so."

Many other entries in the diary were evidently dictated in view of the fact that they were written in excellent script, much different from his own. Because of his partial blindness his own entries were irregular, and each line dropped toward the end. Too, the script was larger and heavier than that of his amanuensis.

Partly blind by this time and suffering all of the afflictions of old age, the General still kept active. He was back at Headquarters every day, maintaining a full schedule. There were more requests than ever for his services at preaching missions, but now his staff handled details.

In 1911 he pursued a program of itineration which kept his aides on their toes. He now traveled by automobile in England and by whatever conveyance was available on the continent. Again he visited Holland, Switzerland, Scandinavia and Italy. His family tried to slow him down but there was no stopping the General. Almost blind and in need of assistance in negotiating the steps of public buildings, he still managed to keep his assistants so busy that they were worn out at the end of a day while he appeared fresh and ready for more conferences.

"It almost seems as if he is indestructible," Bramwell remarked to his wife when reports from meetings on the continent reached him.

"Father *is* indestructible," she replied. "That terrific Booth spirit sustains him."

"That and Salvation," Bramwell suggested. "And I suspect, too, that being General helps some. It's like being the captain of a ship. The sense of responsibility for the lives of hundreds of passengers sustains a skipper in the wildest storms."

"But Father feels a responsibility not for hundreds alone," she reminded him. "If any one man ever carried the burdens of the entire world on his shoulders it's William Booth. You can even see evidences of this in the lines of his face."

"I know," Bramwell agreed, "and it frightens me. I suppose you know that Father wants me to succeed him as General. He informed me of the fact that I'd been selected just before he went overseas. I suspect that I had always hoped I would be his choice, but now that it's impending I'm afraid that I'll not measure up to his expectations."

"You needn't be," she assured him. "When the time comes for you to take over you'll be ready for it."

Shortly afterward the General was back in England. Almost entirely blind, he still managed to tire the young staff officers who were assigned to go with him to Sheffield, Birmingham, and the many other cities which importuned Headquarters for his services.

The Salvation Army post captains seemed to feel a sense of impending loss although they never mentioned it. They wanted the old commander to visit them once more before his voice would be stilled. He was like an army on the march. In the early spring of 1912 he made his last journey overseas. He returned from this visit to the continent singularly depressed. He seemed to sense the world tensions which would make a gigantic war inevitable.

In part the tensions were political but he was so close to the leading politicians, as well as the monarchs, of most of the countries of Europe that he could almost sense what they were thinking and planning.

But, more important still, he noted a lack of spiritual depth in people, in the leaders of the nations and also in the common folk as well.

He remarked to Harold Begbie, who was later to write his biography, "I have an impression that the mass of the people are discovering that there is a great gulf between the profession of love — love which is the core of religion — and the practice in daily life of those activities and self-sacrifices which will ever spring out of love where it exists. Religion has only too widely become a matter of form instead of a living, breathing, active principle — a withered husk, a dead shell — and the man in the street has thrown it away."

For the space of several minutes he pondered the statement which he had just made. Then he added, "I am more confident than ever that Salvation is the only hope for the world. Were it not for Salvation and the Salvation of the Salvation Army, I should think that the probability was that the world was on its way to universal suicide."

On August 20 a fearful thunderstorm occurred, one almost identical to the storm which signaled the passing of his wife. Late that evening the tired old heart stopped beating.

On the night that the end came thousands of people who had never seen him or heard his voice were sleeping in shelters which he had established. In his hostels for women who had been cast out of their own homes thousands of expectant mothers, many of them still girls in their teens, who would bear nameless children, were receiving the tender ministries of devoted Salvation Army nurses because Catherine Booth had seen their helplessness and their need and conceived of these rescue centers which his genius had established.

Eva wanted a quiet funeral.

She explained to Bramwell, "If the doors are thrown open to the populace there will be such a crowd that no building could possibly hold them. And for once we'll keep the Salvation Army band out of it."

"Do you suppose that Father would want the doors closed against anyone?" Bramwell inquired. "And don't you believe that he would want the band?"

"Fife and drum, flute and trumpet?" she asked.

"Yes, everything, including the cymbals. Oh, Eva, we know that the General wouldn't want it for himself, but he would want souls to be won at the service. He'd want Salvation to be proclaimed."

"Yes, I suspect that he would," she acknowledged.

So the General went home to the accompaniment of a brass band. Throngs lined the streets through which the long cortege passed. People craned their necks for a last glimpse of the casket which held the remains of the aged soldier.

Thus, when the General left the scene of his lifelong labors it was to the tune of a Salvation Army hymn played by mass trumpets, fifes, flutes and drums.

And the sermon which was preached on the occasion of his departure was the one which had characterized his own preaching from his boyhood—"Proclaim Salvation throughout the land."